Shakespeare Theatre, Folger Library, Washington, D. C.
Replica of a typical theatre of Shakespeare's time.

TWELFTH NIGHT

With the Famous Temple Notes

by

William Shakespeare

With Copious Notes and Comments by
Henry Norman Hudson, M.A.
Israel Gollancz, M.A.
C. H. Herford, Litt.D.
and One Hundred Other
Eminent Shakespearean Authorities

GROSSET & DUNLAP

Publishers *New York*

PRINTED IN THE UNITED STATES OF AMERICA BY
J. J. LITTLE & IVES COMPANY, NEW YORK

TWELFTH NIGHT;
OR, WHAT YOU WILL

All the unsigned footnotes in this volume are by the writer of the article to which they are appended. The interpretation of the initials signed to the others is: I. G. = Israel Gollancz, M.A.; H. N. H. = Henry Norman Hudson, A.M.; C. H. H. = C. H. Herford, Litt.D.

PREFACE

By Israel Gollancz, M.A.

THE FIRST EDITION

Twelfth Night; or, What You Will, was first printed in the First Folio, where it occupies pages 255–275 in the division of Comedies. There is no record of any earlier edition. The text is singularly free from misprints and corruptions. The list of "Dramatis Personæ" was first given by Rowe, as in the case of many of the plays.

THE DATE OF COMPOSITION

John Manningham, a member of the Middle Temple from January, 1601(–2) to April, 1603, entered in his *Diary*, preserved in the British Museum (MSS. Harleian 5,353),[1] the following statement:—

"Feb. 2, 1601(–2).—At our feast, we had a play called *Twelve Night, or What You Will*. Much like the *Comedy of Errors*, or *Menechmi* in Plautus; but most like and near to that in Italian called *Inganni*. A good practice in it to make the steward believe his lady widowe was in love with him, by counterfeiting as from his lady in general terms, telling him what she liked best in him, and prescribing his gesture in smiling, his apparel, etc., and then when he came to practise, making him believe they took him to be mad," etc. Seeing that *Twelfth Night* is not mentioned by Meres in 1598, and as the play contains fragments of the song "*Farewell, dear heart, since I must needs be gone*," from the *Book of Ayres*, by Robert Jones, first published

[1] *Cp. The Diary of John Manningham*, ed. by John Bruce (*Camden Society*, 1869).

in 1601, the date of composition may with some certainty be assigned to 1601–1602.

TITLE OF THE PLAY

According to Halliwell-Phillipps, *Twelfth Night* was one of four plays acted by Shakespeare's Company, "the Lord Chamberlain's servants," before the Court at Whitehall during the Christmas of 1601–1602; possibly it owed its name to the circumstance that it was first acted as the Twelfth-Night performance on that occasion. Others hold that the name of the play was suggested by its "embodiment of the spirit of the Twelfth-Night sports and revels—a time devoted to festivity and merriment." Its second name, *Or What You Will*, was perhaps given in something of the same spirit as *As You Like It;* it probably implies that the first title has no very special meaning. It has been suggested that the name expresses Shakespeare's indifference to his own production—that it was a sort of farewell to Comedy; in his subsequent plays the tragic element was to predominate. This far-fetched, subtle view of the matter has certainly little to commend it.[1]

THE SOURCES OF THE PLOT

(i) There are at least two Italian plays called *Gl'Inganni* (*The Cheats*), to which Manningham may have referred in his entry as containing incidents resembling those of *Twelfth Night;* one of these plays, by Nicolo Secchi, was printed in 1562; another by Curzio Gonzalo, was first published in 1592. In the latter play the sister, who dresses as a man, and is mistaken for her brother, gives herself the name of Cesare, and it seems likely that we have here the source of Shakespeare's "Cesario." (ii) A third play, however, entitled *Gl'Ingannati* (Venice, 1537), translated by Peacock in 1862, bears a much stronger resemblance to *Twelfth Night;* in its poetical induction,

[1] Marston took the name *What You Will* for a play of his own in 1607.

Il Sacrificio, occurs the name "Malevolti," which is at least suggestive of the name "Malvolio." (iii) The ultimate source of the story is undoubtedly Bandello's *Novelle* (II. 36), whence it passed into Belleforest's *Histoires Tragiques* (Vol. IV, Hist. vii); an English version of the story—probably Shakespeare's original for the general framework of his Comedy—found a place in Barnaby Rich's *Farewell to the Militarye Profession* (1581), where it is styled "*The History of Apollonius and Silla*"; Rich, no doubt, derived it from Cinthio's *Hecatomithi;* Cinthio in his turn was indebted to Bandello. (Rich's *Apollonius and Silla* is printed in Hazlitt's *Shakespeare's Library*, Part 1, Vol. I.)

For the secondary plot, the story of "Malvoglio, that cross-gartered gull," no source exists; Malvolio, Sir Toby Belch, Sir Andrew Aguecheek, Fabian, Feste, and Maria, are wholly Shakespeare's.

BACKWARD LINKS

Twelfth Night, probably the last of the joyous comedies, holding a middle place between *As You Like It* and *All's Well*, suggests noteworthy points of contact with earlier plays: *e. g.* (1) the disguised Viola may well be compared with the disguised Julia in *The Two Gentlemen;* (2) the story of the wreck recalls the similar episode in *The Comedy of Errors;* (3) the whole play is in fact a "Comedy of Errors" arising from mistaken identity; (4) the sentiment of music breathes throughout, as in *The Merchant of Venice*,

> "like the sweet sound
> That breathes upon a bank of violets,
> Stealing and giving odor";

(5) alike, too, in both these plays the faithful friend is named Antonio; (6) in Viola's confession of her secret love (II, iv, 114–122) we have a fuller chord of the note struck in *Love's Labor's Lost;* (7) finally, Sir Andrew is a sort of

elder brother of Cousin Slender, and Sir Toby Belch a near kinsman of Sir John Falstaff.

DURATION OF ACTION

The action of *Twelfth Night* occupies three days, with an interval of three days between the first and second days:—

Day 1. Act I, sc. i–iii. *Interval.*
Day 2. Act I, iv and v; Act II, i–iii.
Day 3. Act II, iv and v; Acts III, IV, and V.

(*cp.* Daniel's *Time-Analysis of Shakespeare's Plays*, Transactions of New Shakespeare Society).

INTRODUCTION

By Henry Norman Hudson, A.M.

Twelfth Night, or What You Will, originally appeared in the folio of 1623, being the thirteenth in the list of Comedies.

In default of positive information, this play was for a long time set down as among the last-written of our author's plays. This opinion was based upon such slight indications gathered from the work itself, as could have no weight but in the absence of other proofs. For example, the word *undertaker* occurs in the play; therefore Tyrwhitt dated the writing of it in 1614, because the term was that year applied to certain men who *undertook* to carry matters in Parliament according to the king's liking; their arts and methods probably being much the same as are used by the lobby members of American legislatures: from which Mr. Verplanck very naturally infers that some of the Anglo-Saxon blood still runs in the veins of our republic. Chalmers, however, supposing that reference was had to the *undertakers* for colonizing Ulster in 1613, assigned the play to that year; and was confirmed therein by the Poet's use of the term Sophy, because the same year Sir Anthony Shirley published his *Travels,* wherein something was said about the Sophy of Persia. Perhaps it did not occur to either of these men that Shakespeare might have taken up the former word from its general use and meaning, not from any special applications of it; these being apt to infer that it was already understood. Malone at first fixed upon 1614, but afterwards changed it to 1607, because the play contains the expression "westward-hoe!" and Dekker's comedy entitled *Westward-Hoe* came out that year; thus assuming that the play gave currency to the phrase, instead of being so named because the phrase was already common. Several other arguments of like sort were urged in favor of this or that date,—arguments for which the best apology is, that the authors had nothing better to build conjecture upon.

All these inferences have been set aside, and their weakness shown, by a recent discovery. In 1828 Mr. Collier, while delving in the "musty records of antiquity" stored away in the Museum,—a work not more toilsome to him than gratifying to us,—met with the following memorandum in a diary preserved among the Harleian Manuscripts:

"Feb. 2, 1602. At our feast we had a play called *Twelve night or what you will*, much like *The Comedy of Errors*, or *Menechmi* in Plautus, but most like and near to that in Italian called *Inganni*. A good practice in it to make the steward believe his lady widow was in love with him, by counterfeiting a letter, as from his lady, in general terms telling him what she liked best in him, and prescribing his gestures, his apparel, etc., and then when he came to practise, making him believe they took him to be mad."

The authorship of the diary containing this precious item was unknown to Mr. Collier, till the Rev. Joseph Hunter ascertained it to be the work of John Manningham, a barrister who was entered at the Middle Temple in 1797. The occasion of the performance thus noted down by Manningham was the feast of the Purification, anciently called Candlemas;—an important link in the course of festivities that used to continue from Christmas to Shrovetide. It would seem that the benchers and members of the several Inns were wont to enrich their convivialities with a course of wit and poetry. And the glorious old Temple is yet standing, where one of Shakespeare's sweetest plays was enjoyed by his contemporaries, at a time when this annual jubilee had rendered their minds congenial and apt, and when Christians have so much cause to be happy and gentle and kind, and therefore to cherish the convivial delectations whence kindness and happiness naturally grow. It scarce need be said that a new grace is added to that ancient and venerable structure by this relic of John Manningham, whom a few strokes of the pen have rendered immortal so long after all other memorials of him had been swept away.

Twelfth Night, therefore, was unquestionably written before 1602. That it was not written before 1598, is probable from its not being spoken of in Meres' *Palladis Tamia*, which came out that year. This probability is heightened almost to certainty by what Maria says of Malvolio in his ludicrous beatitude: "He does smile his face into more lines than are in the new map, with the augmentation of the Indies"; which is evidently an allusion to some contemporary matter, and was so regarded before the date of any such multilineal map was known. It is now ascertained that an English version of Linschoten's *Discourse of Voyages*, containing a map exactly answering to Maria's description, was published in 1598. The allusion can hardly be to anything else; and the words *new map* would seem to infer that the passage was written not long after the appearance of the map in question. Dr. Ulrici and other German critics, thinking *Twelfth Night* to be glanced at in Ben Jonson's *Every Man out of His Humour*, which was first acted in 1599, of course conclude the former play to have been made before that date. But we can discover nothing in Jonson's play, that may be fairly construed as an allusion to *Twelfth Night*.

On the other hand, there is good reason for thinking that the play was not made before 1600. For on June 22 of that year the Privy Council issued an order laying very severe restrictions upon stage performances. After prescribing "that there shall be about the city two houses and no more, allowed to serve for the use of common stage plays; of the which houses, one shall be in Surrey, in the place commonly called *The Bankside*, or thereabouts, and the other in Middlesex"; the order runs thus: "Forasmuch as these stage plays, by the multitude of houses and company of players, have been so frequent, not serving for recreation, but inviting and calling the people daily from their trade and work to misspend their time; it is likewise ordered, that the two several companies of players, assigned unto the two houses allowed, may play each of them in their several houses twice a week, and no oftener: and especially they shall refrain to play on the Sabbath day, upon pain of imprisonment and further penalty. And they shall forbear altogether in the time of Lent, and likewise at such time and times as any extraordinary sickness, or infection of disease, shall appear to be in or about the city." This paper was directed to the Lord Mayor and the Justices of Middlesex and Surrey, "strictly charging them to see to the execution of the same"; and it is plain, that if rigidly enforced it would have amounted almost to a total suppression of play-houses, as the expenses of such establishments could hardly have been met, in the face of so great drawbacks.

In *Twelfth Night*, Act III, sc. i, the Clown says to Viola,—"But, indeed, words are very rascals, since bonds disgraced them"; which strikes us as a probable allusion to the forecited order. Moreover, the Puritans were especially forward and zealous in urging the complaints which put the Privy Council upon issuing this stringent process; and it will hardly be disputed that the character of Malvolio was meant as a satire upon the virtues of that extraordinary people. That the Poet should be somewhat provoked by their instrumentality in bringing about such tight restraints upon the freedom of his art, was certainly natural enough. And surely it is no slight addition to their many claims on our gratitude, that their characteristic violence against the liberty of others, and their innate aptness to think, "because they were virtuous, there should be no more cakes and ale," called forth so rich and withal so good-natured a piece of retaliation. And it is a considerable instance of the Poet's equanimity, that he dealt so fairly by them notwithstanding their vexatious assaults, being content merely to play off upon them the divine witchcraft of his genius. Perhaps it should be remarked, that the order in question, though solicited by the authorities of the city, was not enforced; for even at this early date those righteous magistrates had hit upon the method, which they afterwards plied with such fatal success, of stimulating the complaints of discontented citizens, till orders were taken to remove the alleged grievances, and then letting such orders sleep, lest the enforcing thereof should hush those complaints, and thus lose them their cherished opportunities of annoying the Government.

The critics all agree that some outlines of the serious portion of *Twelfth Night* were drawn, directly or indirectly, from the Italian of Bandello. Several intermediate sources have been pointed out, to which the Poet may have gone; and among them the English of Barnabe Rich, and the French of Belleforest, either of which might well enough have been the true one. Besides these, two Italian plays have lately been discovered, severally entitled *Gl' Inganni* and *Gl' Ingannati*, both also founded upon Bandello, though differing considerably from each other. From the way Manningham speaks, it would seem that *Gl' Inganni* was generally regarded at the time as the original of so much of *Twelfth Night* as was borrowed: yet the play has less of resemblance to this than to any of the other sources mentioned. The point, however, where they all agree, is in having a brother and sister so much alike in person and habit as to be indistinguishable; upon which some of the main incidents are made to turn. In *Gl' Ingannati* there is the further resemblance that Lelia, the heroine, in the disguise of a page serves Flamminio, with whom she is in love, but who is in love with a lady named Isabella; and that Flamminio employs Lelia to plead his cause with Isabella. Mr. Collier thinks it cannot be said with any certainty, that Shakespeare resorted to either of the Italian plays, though he may have read both while considering the best mode of adapting to the stage the incidents of Bandello's novel. As the leading points which they have in common with Shakespeare are much the same in all the authors in question, perhaps we cannot do better than to give an outline or brief abstract of the tale as told by Barnabe Rich; from which a pretty fair estimate of the Poet's obligations may be easily made out. The events of the story, as will be seen, are supposed to have taken place before Constantinople fell into the hands of the Turks.

A certain duke, named Apolonius, had served a year in the wars against the Turk. Returning homewards by sea, he was driven by stress of weather to the isle of Cyprus, where he was well received by Pontus the governor, whose daughter Silla fell so deeply in love with him, that after his departure to Constantinople she forsook home in pursuit of him, having persuaded her man Pedro to go along with her. For security against such perils and injuries as are apt to befall young ladies in her situation, she assumed the dress and name of her brother Silvio, who was absent from home when she left. Coming to Constantinople she inquired out the residence of Apolonius, and presented herself before him, craving to be his servant; and he, being well disposed towards strangers and liking her appearance, took her into his service. Her smooth and gentle behavior soon won his confidence, and her happy diligence in waiting upon him caused her to be advanced above all the rest of his servants in credit and trust.

At this time there dwelt in the city a lady widow named Julina, whose husband had lately died, leaving her large possessions and rich livings, and who, moreover, surpassed all the ladies of Constantinople in beauty. Her attractions of course proved too much for the Duke: he became an earnest suitor to the lady, and employed his new servant to carry his love-tokens and forward his suit. Thus, besides her other afflictions, this piece of disguised sweetness had to endure the greater one of being the instrument to work her own mishap, and of playing the attorney in a cause that made against herself: nevertheless, being altogether desirous to please her master, and caring nothing at all to offend herself, she urged his suit with as much zeal as if it had been her own preferment. But 'twas not long till Silla's sweetness stole through her disguise right into the heart of the lady Julina, who at length got so entangled with the often sight of this sweet temptation, that she fell as much in love with the servant as the master was with herself. Thus things went on, till one day Silla, being sent with a message to the lady, began to solicit very warmly for the Duke, when Julina interrupted her, saying, —Silvio, it is enough that you have said for your master: henceforth either speak for yourself, or say nothing at all.

Meanwhile Silla's brother, the right Silvio indeed, had returned home to Cyprus; and was much grieved to find her missing, whom he loved the more tenderly for that, besides being his own sister, she was so like him in person and feature that no one could distinguish them, save by their apparel. Learning how she had disappeared, and supposing that Pedro had seduced and stolen her away, he vowed to his father that he would not only seek out his sister, but take revenge on the servant. In this mind he departed, and, after seeking through many towns and cities in vain, arrived at Constantinople. One evening, as he was walking for recreation on a pleasant green without the walls of the city, he chanced to meet the lady Julina, who had also gone forth to take the air. Casting her eyes upon Silvio, and thinking him to be the messenger that had so often done enchantment upon her, she drew him aside, and soon courted him into a successful courtship of herself. Of course she was not long in getting tied up beyond the Duke's hope. Now Apolonius had already conceived such a tender friendship for his gentle page as always makes the better part of a genuine love. The appearance of Silla's brother forthwith brings about a full disclosure what and who she is; whereupon the Duke, seeing the lady widow now quite beyond his reach, and learning what precious riches are already his in the form of a serving-man, transfers his heart to Silla, and takes her to his bosom.

The story of Apolonius and Silla, which was evidently made from the matter of Bandello's *Nicuola,* is in a collection entitled Rich's *Farewell to The Military Profession,* which was originally published somewhere between 1578 and 1581, and re-issued in 1606;—a book, says Rich, "containing very pleasant discourses fit for a peaceable time, and gathered together for the only delight of the courteous gentlewomen of England and Ireland." Whether Shakespeare drew directly from this source is very doubtful, there being no verbal resemblances whereby such obligations may usually be traced. Mr. Collier thinks there might be in Shakespeare's time some version of Bandello more like the original than that made by Rich; and that, whether there were or not, the Poet may have gone to the Italian story, since *Le Novelle di Bandello* were very well known in England as early as about the middle of the sixteenth century. It is observable that the lady Julina of Rich's novel, who answers to the Olivia of *Twelfth Night,* is a widow; and that Manningham speaks of Olivia as a "widow." Which suggests that she may have been so represented in the play as acted at the Reader's Feast in 1602; the Poet afterwards making the change: but it seems more likely that the barrister's recollections of Julina got mixed up with his impression of Olivia; the similarity of the stories being apt enough to generate such a confusion.

Thus it appears that the most objectionable, or rather the least admirable points in *Twelfth Night* are precisely those which were least original with the Poet; they being already familiar to his audience, and recommended to his use by the popular literature of the time. Nor is it to be overlooked that his borrowings relate only to the plot of the work, the poetry and character being all his own; and that, here as elsewhere, he used what he took merely as the canvas whereon to pencil out and express the breathing creatures of his mind. As to the comic portion, there is no pretense that any hints or traces of it are to be found in any preceding writer.

Mr. Knight justly remarks upon the singularly composite society here delineated, that while the period of action is undefined, and the scene laid in Illyria, the names of the persons are a mixture of Spanish, Italian, and English. And the discrepancies thence arising he thinks may be best made up, by supposing Duke Orsino to be a Venetian governor of so much of ancient Illyria as remained subject to Venice at the beginning of the seventeenth century; his attendants, Valentine, Curio, etc., as well as Olivia, Malvolio, and Maria, being also Venetians: and Sir Toby and Sir Andrew to be English residents; the former, a maternal uncle to Olivia,—her father, a Venetian count, having married his sister.

This discrepancy in the grouping of the persons, whether so intended or not, very well accords with the spirit in which, or the occasion for which, the title indicates the play to have been written. Twelfth Day, anciently so called as being the twelfth after Christmas, is the day whereon the Church has always kept the feast of "The Epiphany, or the Manifestation of Christ to the Gentiles," by the miraculous leading of a star. So that, in preparing a Twelfth-Night entertainment the idea of fitness might aptly suggest, that national lines and distinctions should be lost in the paramount ties of a common religion: and that people the most diverse in kindred and tongue should draw together in the sentiment of one Lord, one faith, one baptism; their social mirth being thus seasoned with a spicery of heaven, and relishing of universal brotherhood.

The general scope and plan of *Twelfth Night*, as a work of art, is wisely hinted in its second title: all the comic elements being, as it were, thrown out simultaneously and held in a sort of equipoise, thus leaving the readers to fix the preponderance where will best suit their several bent or state of mind; so that within certain limits and conditions each may take the work in *what sense he will*. For where no special prominence is given to one thing, there must needs be wide scope for individual aptitudes and inclinations, and great freedom for everyone to select for virtual prominence such parts as best express or knit in with what is uppermost in his thoughts.

Taking another view of *Twelfth Night* in the light of the same principle, the significancy of the title is further traceable in a peculiar spontaneousness running through the play. Replete as it is with humors and oddities, they all seem to spring up of their own accord; the comic characters being free alike from disguises and pretensions, and seeking merely to let off their inward redundancy; caring not at all whether everybody or nobody sees them, so they may have their whim out, and giving utterance to folly and nonsense simply because they cannot help it. Thus their very deformities have a certain grace, since they are genuine and of nature's planting: absurdity and whimsicality are indigenous to the soil, and shoot up in free, happy luxuriance, from the life that is in them. And by thus setting the characters out in their happiest aspects, the Poet contrives to make them simply ludicrous and diverting, instead of putting upon them the construction of wit or spleen, and thereby making them ridiculous or contemptible. Hence it is that we so readily enter into a sort of fellowship with them; their foibles and follies being shown up in such a spirit of good humor that the subjects themselves would rather join with us in laughing, than be angered or hurt by the exhibition. Moreover, the high and the low are here seen moving in free and familiar intercourse, without any apparent consciousness of their respective ranks: the humors and comicalities of the play keep running and frisking in among the serious parts, to their mutual advantage; the connection between them being of a kind to be felt, not described.

Thus the piece overflows with the genial, free-and-easy spirit of a merry Twelfth Night. Chance, caprice, and intrigue, it is true, are brought together in about equal portions; and their meeting, and crossing, and mutual tripping, cause a deal of perplexity and confusion, defeating the hopes of some, suspending those of others: yet here, as is often the case in actual life, from this conflict of opposites order and happiness spring up as the final result: if what we call accident thwart one cherished purpose, it draws on something better; blighting a full-blown expectation now, to help the blossoming of a nobler one hereafter: and it so happens in the end that all the persons but two either have *what they will*, or grow willing to have what comes to their hand.

If the characters of this play be generally less interesting in themselves than some we meet with elsewhere in the Poet's works, the defect is pretty well made up by the felicitous grouping of them. For broad comic effect, the cluster of which Sir Toby is the center,—all of them drawn in clear yet delicate colors,—is inferior only to the unparalleled assemblage that makes rich the air of Eastcheap. Of Sir Toby himself,—that most whimsical, madcap, frolicsome old toper, so full of antics and fond of sprees, with a plentiful stock of wit and an equal lack of money to keep it in motion,—it is enough to say, with one of the best Shakespearean critics, that "he certainly comes out of the same associations where the Poet saw Falstaff hold his revels"; and that though "not Sir John, nor a fainter sketch of him, yet he has an odd sort of a family likeness to him." Sir Andrew Ague-cheek, the aspiring, lack-a-daisical, self-satisfied echo and sequel of Sir Toby, fitly serves the double purpose of butt and foil to the latter, at once drawing him out and setting him off. Ludicrously proud of the most petty childish irregularities, which, however, his natural fatuity keeps him from acting, and barely suffers him to affect, on this point he reminds us of that impressive imbecility, Abraham Slender; yet not in such sort as to encroach at all upon Slender's province. There can scarce be found a richer piece of diversion than Sir Toby's practice in dandling him out of his money, and paying him off with the odd hope of gaining Olivia's hand. And the funniest of it is, that while Sir Toby thoroughly understands him he has not himself the slightest suspicion what he is, being as confident of his own wit as others are of his want of it.—Malvolio, the self-lovesick Steward, has hardly had justice done him, his bad qualities being indeed just of the kind to defeat the recognition of his good ones. He represents a class of men, not quite extinct even yet, whose leading characteristic is moral vanity and conceit, and who are never satisfied with a law that leaves them free to do right, unless it also give them power to keep others from doing wrong. Of course, therefore, he has too much conscience to mind his own business, and is too pure to tolerate mirth in others, because too much swollen and stiffened with self-love to be merry himself. But here again Mr. Verplanck has spoken so happily that we must needs quote him: "The gravity, the acquirement, the real talent and accomplishment of the man, all made ludicrous, fantastical, and absurd, by his intense vanity, is as true a conception as it is original and droll, and its truth may still be frequently attested by comparison with real Malvolios, to be found everywhere from humble domestic life up to the high places of learning, of the state, and even of the Church."—Maria's quaint stratagem of the letter is evidently for the purpose of disclosing to others what her keener sagacity has discovered long before; and its working lifts her into a model of arch roguish mischievousness, with wit to plan and art to execute whatsoever falls within the scope of such a character. The scenes where the waggish troop, headed by this "noble gull-catcher" and most "excellent devil of wit," bewitch Malvolio into "a contemplative idiot," practicing upon his vanity and conceit until he seems ready to burst with an ecstacy of self-consequence, and they "laugh themselves into stitches" over him, are almost painfully diverting. At length, however, our merriment at seeing him "jet under his advanc'd plumes" passes into pity for his sufferings, and we feel a degree of resentment towards his ingenious persecutors. Doubtless the Poet meant to push the joke upon him so far as to throw our feelings over on his side, and make us take his part. For his character is such that perhaps nothing but excessive reprisals on his vanity could make us do justice to his real worth.—The shrewd, mirth-loving Fabian, who in greedy silence devours up fun, being made so happy by the first tastings, that he dare not laugh lest the noise thereof should lose him the remainder; and the witty-wise Fool, who lives but to jest out philosophy, and moralize the scenes where he moves, by "pinning the pied lappets of his wit to the backs of all about him," complete this strange group of laughing and laughter-moving personages.

Such are the scenes, such the characters that enliven Olivia's mansion during the play; Olivia herself, calm, cheerful, of "smooth, discreet, and stable bearing," hovering about them, sometimes unbending, never losing her dignity among them; often checking, oftener enjoying their merry-makings, and occasionally emerging from her seclusion to be plagued by the Duke's message and bewitched by his messenger: and Viola, always perfect in her part, yet always shrinking from it, appearing among them from time to time on her embassies of love; sometimes a partaker, sometimes a provoker, sometimes the victim, of their mischievous sport.

All this array of comicalities, exhilarating as it is in itself, is rendered doubly so by the frequent changes and playings-in of poetry breathed from the sweetest spots of romance, and which "gives a very echo to the seat where Love is thron'd"; ideas and images of beauty creeping and stealing over the mind with footsteps so soft and delicate that we scarce know what touches us,—the motions of one that had learned to tread

> "As if the wind, not he, did walk,
> Nor prest a flower, nor bow'd a stalk."

Upon this portion of the play Hazlitt remarks in his spirited way,—"Much as we think of catches, and cakes and ale, there is something that we like better. We have a friendship for Sir Toby; we patronize Sir Andrew; we have an understanding with the Clown, a sneaking kindness for Maria and her rogueries; we feel a regard for Malvolio, and sympathize with his gravity, his smiles, his cross-garters, his yellow stockings, and imprisonment: But there is something that excites in us a stronger feeling than all this."

Olivia is a considerable instance how much a fair and candid setting-forth may do to render an ordinary person attractive, and shows that for the home-bred comforts and fireside tenor of life such persons after all are apt to be the best; and it is not a little remarkable that one so willful and perverse on certain points should be so agreeable and interesting upon the whole. If it seem rather naughty in her not to give the Duke a fair chance to try his powers upon her, she gets pretty well paid in falling a victim to the eloquence which her obstinacy stirs up and provokes. Nor is it altogether certain whether her conduct springs from a pride that will not listen where her fancy is not taken, or from an unambitious modesty that prefers not to "match above her degree." Her

> "beauty truly blent, whose red and white
> Nature's own sweet and cunning hand laid on."

saves the credit of the fancy-smitten Duke in such an urgency of suit as might else breed some question of his manliness: and her winning infirmity, as expressed in the sweet violence with which she hastens on "a contract and eternal bond of love" with the astonished and bewildered Sebastian, "that her most jealous and too doubtful soul may live at peace," shows how well the sternness of the brain may be tempered into amiability by the meekness of womanhood. Manifold indeed are the attractions which the Poet has shed upon his heroes and heroines; yet perhaps the learned spirit of the man is more wisely apparent in the home-keeping virtues and unostentatious beauty of his average characters. And surely the contemplation of Olivia may well suggest the question, whether the former be not sometimes too admirable to be so instructive as those whose graces walk more in the light of common day.

Similar thoughts might aptly enough be started by the Duke, who, without any very splendid or striking qualities, manages somehow to be a highly agreeable and interesting person. His character is merely that of an accomplished gentleman, enraptured at the touch of music, and the sport of thick-thronging fancies. It is plain that Olivia has rather enchanted his imagination than won his heart; though he is not himself aware that such is the case. This fancy-sickness, for it appears to be nothing else, naturally renders him somewhat capricious and fantastical, "unstaid and skittish" in his motions; and, but for the exquisite poetry which it inspires him to utter, would rather stir up our mirth than start our sympathy. To use an illustration from another play, Olivia is not so much his Juliet as his Rosaline; and perhaps a secret impression of something like this is the real cause of her rejecting his suit. Accordingly when he sees her placed beyond his hope he has no more trouble about her; but turns and builds a true affection where, during the preoccupancy of his imagination, so many sweet and tender appeals have been made to his heart.

In Viola, what were else not a little scattered are thoroughly composed; her character being the unifying power that draws and binds together the several groups of persons in true dramatic consistency. Love-taught herself, it was for her to teach both the Duke and the Countess how to love: indeed she plays into all the other parts, causing them to embrace and kiss within the compass of her circulation. And yet, like some subtle agency working most where we perceive it least, she does all this in such a way as not to render herself a special prominence in the play.

It is observable that the Poet has left it uncertain whether Viola was in love with the Duke before the assumption of her disguise, or whether her heart was won afterwards by reading "the book even of his secret soul" while wooing another. Nor does it much matter whether her passion were one of the motives, or one of the consequences, of her disguise, since in either case such a man as Olivia describes him to be might well find his way to tougher hearts than hers. But her love has none of the skittishness and unrest which mark the Duke's passion for Olivia: complicated out of all the elements of her richly-gifted, sweetly-tempered nature, it is strong without violence; never mars the innate modesty of her character; is deep as life, tender as infancy, pure, peaceful, and unchangeable as truth.

Mrs. Jameson,—who, with the best right to know what belongs to woman, unites a rare talent for taking others along with her and letting them see the choice things which her gifted, genial eye discerns, and who, in respect of Shakespeare's heroines, has left little for after critics to do but quote her words,—remarks that "in Viola a sweet consciousness of her feminine nature is forever breaking through her masquerade;—she plays her part well, but never forgets, nor allows us to forget, that she is playing a part." And, sure enough, everything about her save her dress "is semblative a woman's part": she has none of the pretty assumption of a pert, saucy, waggish manhood, which so delights us in the Rosalind of *As You Like It;* but she has that which, if not better in itself, is more becoming in her,—"the inward and spiritual grace of modesty" pervading all she does and says. Even in her sweet-witted railleries with the comic characters there is all the while an instinctive drawing back of female delicacy, touching our sympathies, and causing us to feel most deeply what she is, when those with whom she is playing least suspect her to be other than she seems. And the same is true concerning her passion, of which she never so speaks as to compromise in the least the delicacies and proprieties of her sex, yet she lets fall many things from which the Duke easily gathers the true drift and quality of her feelings as soon as he learns what she is.—But the great charm of her character lies in a moral rectitude so perfect as to be a secret unto itself; a clear, serene composure of truth, mingling so freely and smoothly with the issues of life, that while, and perhaps even because, she is herself unconscious of it, she is never once tempted to abuse or shirk her trust, though it be to play the attorney in a cause that makes so much against herself. In this respect she presents a fine contrast to Malvolio, who has much virtue indeed, yet not so much but that the counter-pullings of temptation have rendered him deeply conscious of it, and so drawn him into the vice, at once hateful and ridiculous, of moral pride.

Twelfth Night naturally falls, by internal as well as external notes, into the middle period of the author's productive years. It has no such marks of vast but immature powers as are often to be met with in his earlier plays; nor any of "that intense idiosyncrasy of thought and expression,—that unparalleled fusion of the intellectual with the passionate," which distinguishes his later ones. Everything is calm and quiet, with an air of unruffled serenity and composure about it, as if the Poet had purposely taken to such matter as he could easily mould into graceful and entertaining forms; thus exhibiting none of the crushing muscularity of mind to which the hardest materials afterwards or elsewhere became as limber and pliant as clay in the hands of a potter. Yet the play has a marked severity of taste; the style, though by no means so great as in some others, is singularly faultless; the graces of wit and poetry are distilled into it with indescribable delicacy, as if they came from a hand at once the most plentiful and the most sparing: in short, the work is everywhere replete with "the modest charm of not too much"; its beauty, like that of the heroine, being of the still, deep, retiring sort which it takes some time to find, forever to exhaust, and which can be fully caught only by the reflective imagination in "the quiet and still air of delightful studies." Thus all things are disposed in most happy keeping with each other, and tempered in the blandest proportion of art, as if on purpose to show how

> "Grace, laughter, and discourse may meet,
> And yet the beauty not go less;
> For what is noble should be sweet."

Such, we believe, is pretty nearly our impression of this charming play;—"a drama," as Knight happily describes it, "running over with imagination, and humor, and wit; in which high poetry is welded with intense fun; and we are made to feel that the lofty and the ludicrous in human affairs can only be adequately presented by one who sees the whole from an eagle-height to which ordinary men cannot soar."

culty and without degradation. It is with like uncritical, though not unwondering, acquiescence that Sebastian receives his good fortune; and it is the naturalness of this, as a point of twin likeness, that reconciles us to it, and thus saves him from any appearance of dullness on the one hand, or duplicity on the other.—LLOYD, *Critical Essays*.

OLIVIA

The Countess Olivia forms a pendant to the Duke; she, like him, is full of yearning melancholy. With an ostentatious exaggeration of sisterly love, she has vowed to pass seven whole years veiled like a nun, consecrating her whole life to sorrow for her dead brother. Yet we find in her speeches no trace of this devouring sorrow; she jests with her household, and rules it ably and well, until, at the first sight of the disguised Viola, she flames out into passion, and, careless of the traditional reserve of her sex, takes the most daring steps to win the supposed youth. She is conceived as an unbalanced character, who passes at a bound from exaggerated hatred for all worldly things to total forgetfulness of her never-to-be-forgotten sorrow. Yet she is not comic like Phebe; for Shakespeare has indicated that it is the Sebastian type, foreshadowed in the disguished Viola, which is irresistible to her; and Sebastian, we see, at once requites the love which his sister had to reject. Her utterance of her passion, moreover, is always poetically beautiful.

Yet while she is sighing in vain for Viola, she necessarily appears as though seized with a mild erotic madness, similar to that of the Duke: and the folly of each is parodied in a witty and delightful fashion by Malvolio's entirely ludicrous love for his mistress, and vain confidence that she returns it. Olivia feels and says this herself, where she exclaims (III, iv)—

> "Go call him hither.—I am as mad as he
> If sad and merry madness equal be."

—BRANDES, *William Shakespeare.*

Olivia, at first sight, seems scarcely suited to attract, except by the power of contrast, the sentimental nature of Orsino. Young and beautiful she indeed is, but the serious tendency of her mind has been aggravated by the death in quick succession of her father and her brother, and she has shut herself up for seven years in cloistral seclusion to nurse her grief. Everything in her surroundings bears witness to her austere temper. Her household is governed by a puritanical steward on rigid principles of order, and though her unusually strong sense of the ties of relationship leads her to entertain a roystering kinsman, she seeks to confine his licence within endurable limits. She is an enemy to all false show, inward or outward. No paint contributes to the red and white of her cheeks, and she scorns overstrained praise or "lowly feigning" from the lips of others. It is not strange that this "mouse of virtue," as the Fool aptly calls her, whose very seal bears the image of the chaste Lucrece, should shrink back in disgust from the cloying incense of Orsino's adoration, and (in a phrase that drops naturally from the mouth of a recluse) should term his love "a heresy." But the icy manner in which she rejects his addresses shows that she pushes austerity to a point where it becomes indifference to the sufferings of others, and she pays a full penalty when, at the first sight of the disguised Viola, her heart overflows with a passion for the servant, as intense and as fruitless as that of the master for herself.—Boas, *Shakspere and his Predecessors.*

MALVOLIO

Malvolio, the steward of Olivia's household, is prized by that lady for his grave and punctilious disposition. He discharges his office carefully and in a tone of some superiority, for his mind is above his estate. At some time in his life he has read cultivated books, knows the theory of Pythagoras concerning the transmigration of the soul, but thinks more nobly of the soul and no way approves that opinion. His gentility, though a little rusted and obsolete, is like a Sunday suit which nobody thinks of rallying. He wears it well, and his mistress cannot afford to treat him exactly as a servant; in fact, she has occasionally dropped good-natured phrases which he has interpreted into a special partiality: for Quixotic conceits can riot about inside of his stiff demeanor. This proneness to fantasy increases the touchiness of a man of reserve. He can never take a joke, and his climate is too inclement to shelter humor. Souls must be at blood-heat, and brains must expand with it like a blossom, before humor will fructify. He wonders how Olivia can tolerate the clown. "I protest," he says, "I take these wise men, that crow so at these set kind of fools, to be no better than the fools' zanies." Olivia hits the difficulty when she replies, "Oh, you are sick of self-love, and taste with a distempered appetite." Perhaps he thinks nobly of the soul because he so profoundly respects his own, and carries it upon stilts over the heads of the servants and Sir Toby and Sir Andrew.

Imagine this saturnine and self-involved man obliged to consort daily with Sir Toby, who brings his hand to the buttery-bar before breakfast, and who hates going to bed "as an unfilled can," unless no more drink is forthcoming; an irascible fellow, too, and all the more tindery because continually dry. He has Sir Andrew Aguecheek for a boon companion, who says of himself that sometimes he has no more wit than a Christian, or than an ordinary man. When he is not in liquor he is fuddled with inanity, and chirps and skips about, deluding himself with the notion that Olivia will receive his addresses. Sir Toby, to borrow money of him, fosters the notion, and flatters his poor tricks. Then there is that picador of a clown, who plants in Malvolio's thin skin a perfect quickset of barbed quips, and sends him lowering around the mansion which these roisterers have turned into a tavern. The other servant, Fabian, has a grudge against him for interfering with a bear-baiting he was interested in; for

Malvolio was one of those Puritans who frowned upon that sport, as Macaulay said, not because it worried the bear, but because it amused the men. The steward was right when he informed this precious set that they were idle, shallow things, and he was not of their element. No doubt he is the best man of the lot. But he interrupts their carousing at midnight in such a sour and lofty way that we are entertained to hear their drunken chaffing, and we call to Maria for another stoup, though they have had too much already; but a fresh exposition of dryness always sets in when such a virtue as Malvolio's tries to wither us. However, he becomes the object of their animosity, and they work in his distemper to make him ridiculous.—WEISS, *Wit, Humor, and Shakespeare.*

SIR ANDREW

The reverse to this caricature [Malvolio] is the squire Sir Andrew. He is a melancholy picture of what man would be without any self-love, the source indeed of so many weaknesses. To this straight-haired country squire, life consists only in eating and drinking; eating beef, he himself fears, has done harm to his wit; in fact, he is stupid even to silliness, totally deprived of all passion, and thus of all self-love or self-conceit. He looks up to the awkward Sir Toby, as well as to the adroit fool, as paragons of urbane manners, and seeks to copy their phraseology; he is the parrot and the utterly thoughtless echo of Sir Toby; he thinks to have everything, to be and to have been all that Sir Toby was and had; he repeats his words and imitates him, without even understanding what he says. The dissolute Sir Toby has brought him forward as a suitor for Olivia, that he may fleece him; but the poor suitor himself believes not in his success, and is ever on the point of departing. He despairs of his manners, and the cold sweat stands on his brow if his business is only with the chamber-maid. He repeats indeed after Sir Toby that he too was adored once; but we see, whilst he

velopment of the action, not the nucleus and gravitating point of the whole.—ULRICI, *Shakespeare's Dramatic Art.*

UNITY OF PERSONS AND PLACE

What Bassanio is for the organic unity of *The Merchant of Venice,* Olivia is for *Twelfth Night.* In neither of the two plots is she the chief character, but merely a very prominent one; to win her hand is the mainspring of one, whereby a chance is given to Viola to reveal her feminine advantages, as it is also of the other, which involves Malvolio's humiliation. How important she is to the establishment of the artistic whole will be noted if we were to put another character in her place as the aim of Malvolio's ambition. Should the aspirations of the steward extend beyond the house of his mistress, his discomforture elsewhere follows, and the artistic unity of the plot is lost as well as our own interest, and, in fact, we have enclosed two comedies in one frame. To guard against the impression that we have here a mere unity of persons, there is the unity of place; there are only six short scenes, secondary components of the composition, and one chief scene (Act II, sc. iv) which are not laid in Olivia's house. Through this arrangement not only do actors in both plots come in continuous touch with each other, but the plots themselves define each other and interlace.

Just as the haughty Olivia excites the aspirations of the narrow prosaic Malvolio, so Viola is brought down from romantic heights to common daily life by the episode of the duel, which also serves to reveal the pusillanimity of Sir Andrew. Malvolio's mad presumption was fostered by the favored position which his liberal unsuspicious mistress gave him near her person; and his hopes were nourished by the persistent rejection to which even such a brilliant wooer as the Duke had to submit. And never could Sir Toby have kindled in Sir Andrew's soul such murderous designs had not Viola been the messenger of love from a powerful rival. Sebastian, too, could not have won Olivia until he had proved his valor on the two foolish knights.—Conrad, *Preuss. Jahrbücher.*

A PERFECT CREATION

Notwithstanding minor discrepancies, I may call attention to the marvelous oneness of *Twelfth Night;* there is nothing in excess; at every point drama and poem mingle and are transfigured; the notes of wisdom and merriment, tenderness and raillery, joy and sadness melt into the controlling harmony of love; the play indeed is among those perfect creations in which faultless form is vitalized by faultless spirit.—Luce, *Handbook to Shakespeare's Works.*

THE SPIRIT OF THE PLAY

This comedy is pervaded with the spirit of literature and gentility. It is lifted above the working-day world into a sphere of ease, culture, and good-breeding. Its characters are votaries of pleasure in different degrees, from the exercise of the imagination, which, after all, are but pleasures of the sense at second-hand. Besides the air of elegance it possesses, it is filled to the brim and overflowing with the spirit that seeks to enjoy this world without one thought or aspiration beyond. It jumps the hereafter entirely. Every scene of it glows with the warmth and sunshine of physical enjoyment. It places before us the sensual man, with his fondness of cheer, his cakes and ale, his delights of the eye and ear, his pleasure in pastime and sport, his high estimation of a good leg and a good voice, in short, of all that can gratify the sense, win favor, or conduce to worldly advantage.—Ruggles, *Method of Shakespeare as an Artist.*

THE GENIAL TEMPER OF THE PLAY

It is scarcely necessary for us to enter into any analysis of the plot of this charming comedy, or attempt any dissection of its characters, for the purpose of opening to the reader new sources of enjoyment. It is impossible, we think, for one of ordinary sensibility to read through the first act without yielding himself up to the genial temper in which the entire play is written. "The sunshine of the breast," spreads its rich purple light over the whole champain and penetrates into every thicket and every dingle. From the first line to the last—from the Duke's

"That strain again;—it had a dying fall,"

to the Clown's

"With hey, ho, the wind and the rain,"—

there is not a thought, or a situation, that is not calculated to call forth pleasurable feelings. The love-melancholy of the Duke is a luxurious abandonment to one pervading impression—not a fierce and hopeless contest with one o'ermastering passion. It delights to lie "canopied with bowers,"—to listen to "old and antique" songs, which dally with its "innocence,"—to be "full of shapes," and "high fantastical." The love of Viola is the sweetest and tenderest emotion that ever informed the heart of the purest and most graceful of beings with a spirit almost divine. Perhaps in the whole range of Shakespeare's poetry there is nothing which comes more unbidden into the mind, and always in connection with some image of the ethereal beauty of the utterer, than Viola's "she never told her love." The love of Olivia, willful as it is, is not in the slightest degree repulsive. With the old stories before him, nothing but the refined delicacy of Shakespeare's conception of the female character could have redeemed Olivia from approaching to the anti-feminine. But as it is we pity her, and we rejoice with her. These are what may be called the serious characters, because they are the vehicles for what we emphatically call the poetry of the play. But the comic characters are to us equally poetical —that is, they appear to us not mere copies of the representatives of temporary or individual follies, but embodyings of the universal comic, as true and as fresh to-day as they were two centuries and a half ago. Malvolio is to our minds as poetical as Don Quixote; and we are by no means sure that Shakespeare meant the poor cross-gartered Steward *only* to be laughed at, any more than Cervantes did the knight of the rueful countenance. He meant us to pity him, as Olivia and the Duke pitied him; for, in truth, the delusion by which Malvolio was wrecked, only passed out of the romantic into the comic through the manifestation of the vanity of the character in reference to his situation. But if we laugh at Malvolio we are not to laugh ill-naturedly, for the poet has conducted all the mischief against him in a spirit in which there is no real malice at the bottom of the fun. Sir Toby is a most genuine character,—one given to strong potations and boisterous merriment; but with a humor about him perfectly irresistible. His *abandon* to the instant opportunity of laughing at and with others is something so thoroughly English, that we are not surprised the poet gave him an English name. And like all genuine humorists Sir Toby must have his butt. What a trio is presented in that glorious scene of the second act, where the two Knights and the Clown "make the welkin dance";—the humorist, the fool, and the philosopher!—for Sir Andrew is the fool, and the Clown is the philosopher. We hold the Clown's epilogue song to be the most philosophical Clown's song upon record; and a treatise might be written upon its wisdom. It is the history of a life, from the condition of "a little tiny boy," through "man's estate," to decaying age—"when I came unto my bed"; and the conclusion is, that what is true of the individual is true of the species, and what was of yesterday was of generations long past away—for

"A great while ago the world begun."

—KNIGHT, *Pictorial Shakespeare.*

SHAKESPEARE'S COMIC GENIUS

This is justly considered as one of the most delightful of Shakespeare's comedies. It is full of sweetness and pleasantry. It is perhaps too good-natured for comedy. It has little satire, and no spleen. It aims at the ludicrous rather than the ridiculous. It makes us laugh at the follies of mankind, not despise them, and still less bear any ill-will towards them. Shakespeare's comic genius resembles the bee rather in its power of extracting sweets from weeds or poisons, than in leaving a sting behind it. He gives the most amusing exaggeration of the prevailing foibles of his characters, but in a way that they themselves, instead of being offended at, would almost join in to humor; he rather contrives opportunities for them to show themselves off in the happiest lights, than renders them contemptible in the perverse construction of the wit or malice of others.—HAZLITT, *Characters of Shakespeare's Plays.*

TWELFTH NIGHT;
OR, WHAT YOU WILL

DRAMATIS PERSONÆ

ORSINO, *Duke of Illyria*
SEBASTIAN, *brother to Viola*
ANTONIO, *a sea captain, friend to Sebastian*
A Sea Captain, *friend to Viola*
VALENTINE, } *gentlemen attending on the Duke*
CURIO, }
SIR TOBY BELCH, *uncle to Olivia*
SIR ANDREW AGUECHEEK
MALVOLIO, *steward to Olivia*
FABIAN, } *servants to Olivia*
FESTE, *a clown,* }

OLIVIA
VIOLA
MARIA, *Olivia's woman*

Lords, Priests, Sailors, Officers, Musicians, and other Attendants

SCENE: *A city in Illyria, and the sea coast near it*

SYNOPSIS

By J. Ellis Burdick

ACT I

Orsino, Duke of Illyria, is suing for the hand of Olivia, a noble lady of the same place. Into his service enters Viola, a young gentlewoman of Messaline, who has become separated from her twin brother Sebastian by shipwreck and has donned male attire. These twins are so much alike that only by their dress could they be told apart. Viola as Cesario finds favor with the Duke and is sent by him to court Olivia for him. This she does so well that the lady gives her love to the supposed youth instead of to the master.

ACT II

Olivia sends a ring and message to Viola, who realizes what has happened to the lady and pities her. She herself has fallen in love with the Duke and is, of course, obliged to conceal her passion. Malvolio, steward to Olivia, is so conceited that his fellow-servants plan a practical joke on him and write him a letter full of love-expressions which he believes to come from his mistress.

ACT III

Olivia's love for the page becomes so intense that she openly confesses it to Viola who answers her "I have but one heart, one bosom, and one truth, and that no woman has." One of Olivia's other suitors, Sir Andrew Aguecheek, is jealous of the attention and favor the lady shows the page and challenges Viola. The duel is stopped ere it began by the timely arrival of some officers of the law. In the meantime Malvolio's actions are so ridiculous that Olivia believes him insane and has him locked in a dark room.

ACT IV

Viola's brother Sebastian had also been rescued at the time of the shipwreck. He now arrives in Illyria and being met on the street by Sir Andrew is mistaken by that gentleman for Viola and the fight is renewed. This time it is Olivia who stops the duel, thinking that Sebastian is the page Cesario. She invites him home with her and is delighted when instead of rejecting her love as in the past he returns it, and they are secretly married by a priest.

ACT V

Olivia meets Viola on the street in the company of the Duke and calls her husband. Viola denies the title but the priest who had married Olivia and Sebastian supports Olivia's claims. The Duke is angry at what he believes is treachery on the part of his page. The situation is relieved by the entrance of Sebastian. Brother and sister are united again; the Duke finds the attraction which the page had always inspired in him, ripens into love when he knows she is a woman; and Olivia finds that she has now a sister as well as a husband. The cause of Malvolio's insanity is discovered and he is released from his prison.

TWELFTH NIGHT;
OR, WHAT YOU WILL

ACT FIRST

Scene I

An apartment in the Duke's palace.

Enter Duke, Curio, and other Lords; Musicians attending.

Duke. If music be the food of love, play on;
Give me excess of it, that, surfeiting,
The appetite may sicken, and so die.
That strain again! it had a dying fall:
O, it came o'er my ear like the sweet sound,
That breathes upon a bank of violets,
Stealing and giving odor! Enough; no more:

5. *"sound"*; so the Folios; Pope changed it to *"south,"* and editors have generally accepted this emendation, but it seems unnecessary: Grant White appropriately asks, "Did Pope, or the editors who have followed him, ever lie musing on the sward at the edge of a wood, and hear the low sweet hum of the summer air, as it kissed the coyly-shrinking wild flowers upon the banks, and passed on loaded with fragrance from the sweet salute?"—I. G.

7. *"and giving odor"*; Milton seems to have had this in his eye when he wrote the richly-freighted lines:

"Now gentle gales,
Fanning their odoriferous wings, dispense
Native perfumes, and whisper whence they stole
Those balmy spoils."—H. N. H.

'Tis not so sweet now as it was before.
O spirit of love, how quick and fresh art thou!
That, notwithstanding thy capacity 10
Receiveth as the sea, nought enters there,
Of what validity and pitch soe'er,
But falls into abatement and low price,
Even in a minute! so full of shapes is fancy,
That it alone is high fantastical.

Cur. Will you go hunt, my lord?

Duke. What, Curio?

Cur. The hart.

Duke. Why, so I do, the noblest that I have:
O, when mine eyes did see Olivia first,
Methought she purged the air of pestilence! 20
That instant was I turn'd into a hart;
And my desires, like fell and cruel hounds,
E'er since pursue me.

Enter Valentine.

How now! what news from her?

Val. So please my lord, I might not be admitted;
But from her handmaid do return this answer:

12. *"pitch";* high worth.—C. H. H.

22. *"like fell and cruel hounds";* referring to the story of Actæon.—I. G.

Shakespeare seems to think men cautioned against too great familiarity with forbidden beauty by the fable of Actæon, who saw Diana naked, and was torn to pieces by his hounds; as a man indulging his eyes or his imagination with a view of a woman he cannot gain, has his heart torn with incessant longing. An interpretation far more elegant and natural than Lord Bacon's, who, in his *Wisdom of the Ancients,* supposes this story to warn us against inquiring into the secrets of princes, by showing that those who know that which for reasons of state ought to be concealed will be detected and destroyed by their own servants.—H. N. H.

The element itself, till seven years' heat,
Shall not behold her face at ample view;
But, like a cloistress, she will veiled walk
And water once a day her chamber round
With eye-offending brine: all this to season 30
A brother's dead love, which she would keep fresh
And lasting in her sad remembrance.

Duke. O, she that hath a heart of that fine frame
To pay this debt of love but to a brother,
How will she love, when the rich golden shaft
Hath kill'd the flock of all affections else
That live in her; when liver, brain and heart,
These sovereign thrones, are all supplied, and fill'd
Her sweet perfections with one self king!
Away before me to sweet beds of flowers: 40
Love-thoughts lie rich when canopied with bowers. [*Exeunt.*

26. *"till seven years' heat"*; for seven summers.—C. H. H.

30. *"to season"*; that is, preserve. The Poet elsewhere uses *season* in this sense. Thus in *Romeo and Juliet,* Act ii. sc. 3:

> "Jesu Maria! what a deal of *brine*
> Hath wash'd thy sallow cheeks for Rosaline!
> How much salt water thrown away in waste,
> To *season* love!"—H. N. H.

32. *"remembrance"*; four syllables.—C. H. H.

35. *"shaft"*; *i. e.* of Cupid.—C. H. H.

38. *"all supplied, and filled"*; the comma after *"supplied"* is not in the Folio: its insertion simplifies the lines. Others leave the Folio reading, but bracket *"her sweet perfections"* in the next line; making them appositional to "*thrones.*"—I. G.

Scene II

The sea-coast.

Enter Viola, a Captain, and Sailors.

Vio. What country, friends, is this?
Cap. This is Illyria, lady.
Vio. And what should I do in Illyria?
My brother he is in Elysium.
Perchance he is not drown'd: what think you, sailors?
Cap. It is perchance that you yourself were saved.
Vio. O my poor brother! and so perchance may he be.
Cap. True, madam: and, to comfort you with chance,
Assure yourself, after our ship did split,
When you and those poor number saved with you 10
Hung on our driving boat, I saw your brother,
Most provident in peril, bind himself,
Courage and hope both teaching him the practice,
To a strong mast that lived upon the sea;
Where, like Arion on the dolphin's back,
I saw him hold acquaintance with the waves
So long as I could see.
Vio. For saying so, there 's gold:

10. *"Number"* is here used as the plural, so that *those* should not be changed to *that,* as it usually is.—H. N. H.

15. *"Arion on the dolphin's back";* the Folios misprint *"Orion"* for *"Arion."*—I. G.

Mine own escape unfoldeth to my hope,
Whereto thy speech serves for authority, 20
The like of him. Know'st thou this country?

Cap. Aye, madam, well; for I was bred and born
Not three hours' travel from this very place.

Vio. Who governs here?

Cap. A noble Duke, in nature as in name.

Vio. What is his name?

Cap. Orsino.

Vio. Orsino! I have heard my father name him:
He was a bachelor then.

Cap. And so is now, or was so very late; 30
For but a month ago I went from hence,
And then 'twas fresh in murmur,—as, you know,
What great ones do the less will prattle of,—
That he did seek the love of fair Olivia.

Vio. What 's she?

Cap. A virtuous maid, the daughter of a count
That died some twelvemonth since; then leaving her
In the protection of his son, her brother,
Who shortly also died: for whose dear love,
They say, she hath abjured the company 40
And sight of men.

Vio. O that I served that lady,
And might not be delivered to the world,
Till I had made mine own occasion mellow,
What my estate is!

21. *"The like of him"*; a similar escape in his case.—C. H. H.
42. *"delivered"*; made known.—C. H. H.
44. *"What my estate is"*; that is, "I wish I might not be *made*

Cap. That were hard to compass;
Because she will admit no kind of suit,
No, not the Duke's.

Vio. There is a fair behavior in thee, captain;
And though that nature with a beauteous wall
Doth oft close in pollution, yet of thee
I will believe thou hast a mind that suits 50
With this thy fair and outward character.
I prithee, and I 'll pay thee bounteously,
Conceal me what I am, and be my aid
For such disguise as haply shall become
The form of my intent. I 'll serve this Duke:
Thou shalt present me as an eunuch to him:
It may be worth thy pains; for I can sing,
And speak to him in many sorts of music,
That will allow me very worth his service.
What else may hap to time I will commit; 60
Only shape thou thy silence to my wit.

Cap. Be you his eunuch, and your mute I 'll be:
When my tongue blabs, then let mine eyes not
see.

Vio. I thank thee: lead me on. [*Exeunt.*

public to the world, with regard to the state of my birth and fortune, till I have gained a *ripe opportunity* for my design."—H. N. H.

56. *"as an eunuch to him"*; this plan of Viola's was not pursued, as it would have been inconsistent with the plot of the play. She was presented as a *page*, not as an *eunuch*.—H. N. H.

Scene III

Olivia's house.

Enter Sir Toby Belch and Maria.

Sir. To. What a plague means my niece, to take the death of her brother thus? I am sure care 's an enemy to life.

Mar. By my troth, Sir Toby, you must come in earlier o' nights: your cousin, my lady, takes great exceptions to your ill hours.

Sir. To. Why, let her except, before excepted.

Mar. Aye, but you must confine yourself within the modest limits of order. 10

Sir To. Confine! I 'll confine myself no finer than I am: these clothes are good enough to drink in; and so be these boots too: an they be not, let them hang themselves in their own straps.

Mar. That quaffing and drinking will undo you: I heard my lady talk of it yesterday; and of a foolish knight that you brought in one night here to be her wooer.

Sir. To. Who, Sir Andrew Aguecheek? 20

Mar. Aye, he.

Sir To. He 's as tall a man as any 's in Illyria.

Mar. What 's that to the purpose?

Sir To. Why, he has three thousand ducats a year.

Mar. Aye, but he 'll have but a year in all these ducats: he 's a very fool and a prodigal.

Sir To. Fie, that you 'll say so! he plays o' the viol-de-gamboys, and speaks three or four languages word for word without book, and hath all the good gifts of nature. 30

Mar. He hath indeed, almost natural: for besides that he 's a fool, he 's a great quarreler: and but that he hath the gift of a coward to allay the gust he hath in quarreling, 'tis thought among the prudent he would quickly have the gift of a grave.

Sir To. By this hand, they are scoundrels and subtractors that say so of him. Who are they? 40

Mar. They that add, moreover, he 's drunk nightly in your company.

Sir To. With drinking healths to my niece: I 'll drink to her as long as there is a passage in my throat and drink in Illyria: he 's a coward and a coystrill that will not drink to my niece till his brains turn o' the toe like a parish-top. What, wench! Castiliano vulgo; for here comes Sir Andrew Agueface. 50

Enter Sir Andrew Aguecheek.

Sir And. Sir Toby Belch! how now, Sir Toby Belch!

Sir To. Sweet Sir Andrew!

Sir And. Bless you, fair shrew.

Mar. And you too, sir.

Sir To. Accost, Sir Andrew, accost.

Sir And. What 's that?

Sir To. My niece's chambermaid.

Sir And. Good Mistress Accost, I desire better acquaintance. 60

Mar. My name is Mary, sir.

Sir And. Good Mistress Mary Accost,—

Sir To. You mistake, knight: 'accost' is front her, board her, woo her, assail her.

Sir And. By my troth, I would not undertake her in this company. Is that the meaning of 'accost'?

Mar. Fare you well, gentlemen.

Sir To. An thou let part so, Sir Andrew, would thou mightst never draw sword again. 70

Sir And. An you part so, mistress, I would I might never draw sword again. Fair lady, do you think you have fools in hand?

Mar. Sir, I have not you by the hand.

Sir And. Marry, but you shall have; and here 's my hand.

Mar. Now, sir, 'thought is free': I pray you, bring your hand to the buttery-bar and let it drink.

Sir And. Wherefore, sweetheart? what 's your metaphor? 80

56. Sir Toby speaks more learnedly than intelligibly here, using *accost* in its original sense. The word is from the French *accoster,* to come *side by side,* or to *approach. Accost* is seldom used thus, which accounts for Sir Andrew's mistake.—H. N. H.

78. *"bring your hand to the buttery-bar and let it drink";* "a proverbial phrase among Abigails, to ask at once for a kiss and a present" (Kenrick).—I. G.

Mar. It 's dry, sir.

Sir And. Why, I think so: I am not such an ass but I can keep my hand dry. But what 's your jest?

Mar. A dry jest, sir.

Sir And. Are you full of them?

Mar. Aye, sir, I have them at my fingers' ends: marry, now I let go your hand, I am barren. [*Exit.*

Sir To. O knight, thou lackest a cup of canary: when did I see thee so put down? 90

Sir And. Never in your life, I think; unless you see canary put me down. Methinks sometimes I have no more wit than a Christian or an ordinary man has: but I am a great eater of beef and I believe that does harm to my wit.

Sir To. No question.

Sir And. An I thought that, I 'ld forswear it. I 'll ride home to-morrow, Sir Toby. 100

Sir To. Pourquoi, my dear knight?

Sir And. What is 'pourquoi'? do or not do? I would I had bestowed that time in the tongues that I have in fencing, dancing and bear-baiting: O, had I but followed the arts!

Sir To. Then hadst thou had an excellent head of hair.

86. *"A dry jest"*; a dull one; wit being conceived as a moisture or "humor" of the brain.—C. H. H.

106. *"Then hadst thou had an excellent head of hair"*; Sir Toby evidently plays upon *"tongues"* and *"tongs"* (*i. e.* curling-tongs).—I. G.

Sir And. Why, would that have mended my hair?

Sir To. Past question; for thou seest it will not curl by nature. 110

Sir And. But it becomes me well enough, does 't not?

Sir To. Excellent; it hangs like flax on a distaff; and I hope to see a housewife take thee between her legs and spin it off.

Sir And. Faith, I 'll home to-morrow, Sir Toby: your niece will not be seen; or if she be, it 's four to one she 'll none of me: the count himself here hard by woos her. 120

Sir To. She 'll none o' the count: she 'll not match above her degree, neither in estate, years, nor wit; I have heard her swear 't. Tut, there 's life in 't, man.

Sir And. I 'll stay a month longer. I am a fellow o' the strangest mind i' the world; I delight in masques and revels sometimes altogether.

Sir To. Art thou good at these kickshawses, knight? 130

Sir And. As any man in Illyria, whatsoever he be, under the degree of my betters; and yet I will not compare with an old man.

111. *"curl by nature"*; the original has *cool my nature*. The credit of the happy emendation belongs to Theobald.—H. N. H.

133. *"an old man"*; Theobald proposed to read *"a noble man,"* taking the allusion to be to Orsino. Clarke explains *"an old man"* as "a man of experience"; "the word *old,*" he adds, "gives precisely that absurd effect of refraining from competing in dancing, fencing, etc., with exactly the antagonist incapacitated by age over whom Sir Andrew might hope to prove his superiority."—I. G.

Sir To. What is thy excellence in a galliard, knight?

Sir And. Faith, I can cut a caper.

Sir To. And I can cut the mutton to 't.

Sir And. And I think I have the back-trick simply as strong as any man in Illyria.

Sir To. Wherefore are these things hid? wherefore have these gifts a curtain before 'em? are they like to take dust, like Mistress Mall's picture? why dost thou not go to church in a galliard and come home in a coranto? My very walk should be a jig; I would not so much as make water but in a sink-a-pace. What dost thou mean? Is it a world to hide virtues in? I did think, by the excellent constitution of thy leg, it was formed under the star of a galliard. 140 150

Sir And. Aye, 'tis strong, and it does indifferent well in a flame-colored stock. Shall we set about some revels?

Sir To. What shall we do else? were we not born under Taurus?

Sir And. Taurus! That 's sides and heart.

Sir To. No, sir; it is legs and thighs. Let me see thee caper: ha! higher: ha, ha! excellent! [*Exeunt.*

146. *"sink-a-pace"*; "cinque pas," dance of five paces.—C. H. H.

156. *"That's sides and heart"*; Sir Andrew and Sir Toby are wrong in the parts assigned to Taurus in the old astrological figures of the human body. Taurus was supposed to govern the neck and throat.—I. G.

Scene IV

The Duke's palace.

Enter Valentine, and Viola in man's attire.

Val. If the Duke continue these favors towards you, Cesario, you are like to be much advanced: he hath known you but three days, and already you are no stranger.

Vio. You either fear his humor or my negligence, that you call in question the continuance of his love: is he inconstant, sir, in his favors?

Val. No, believe me.

Vio. I thank you. Here comes the count. 10

Enter Duke, Curio, and Attendants.

Duke. Who saw Cesario, ho?

Vio. On your attendance, my lord; here.

Duke. Stand you a while aloof. Cesario,
Thou know'st no less but all; I have unclasp'd
To thee the book even of my secret soul:
Therefore, good youth, address thy gait unto
her;
Be not denied access, stand at her doors,
And tell them, there thy fixed foot shall grow
Till thou have audience.

Vio. Sure, my noble lord,

3. *"three days"*; Mr. Daniel points out in his "Time-Analysis" that this statement is inconsistent with the Duke's words in V. i. 106, *"Three months this youth hath tended upon me."*—I. G.

5. *"humor"*; fickleness.—C. H. H.

If she be so abandon'd to her sorrow 20
As it is spoke, she never will admit me.

Duke. Be clamorous and leap all civil bounds
Rather than make unprofited return.

Vio. Say I do speak with her, my lord, what then?

Duke. O, then unfold the passion of my love,
Surprise her with discourse of my dear faith:
It shall become thee well to act my woes;
She will attend it better in thy youth
Than in a nuncio's of more grave aspect.

Vio. I think not so, my lord.

Duke. Dear lad, believe it; 30
For they shall yet belie thy happy years,
That say thou art a man; Diana's lip
Is not more smooth and rubious; thy small pipe
Is as the maiden's organ, shrill and sound;
And all is semblative a woman's part.
I know thy constellation is right apt
For this affair. Some four or five attend him;
All, if you will; for I myself am best
When least in company. Prosper well in this,
And thou shalt live as freely as thy lord, 40
To call his fortunes thine.

Vio. I'll do my best
To woo your lady: [*Aside*] yet, a barful strife!
Whoe'er I woo, myself would be his wife.

[*Exeunt.*

36. *"thy constellation"*; the stars under which you were born.—C. H. H.

Scene V

Olivia's house.

Enter Maria and Clown.

Mar. Nay, either tell me where thou hast been, or I will not open my lips so wide as a bristle may enter in way of thy excuse: my lady will hang thee for thy absence.

Clo. Let her hang me: he that is well hanged in this world needs to fear no colors.

Mar. Make that good.

Clo. He shall see none to fear.

Mar. A good lenten answer: I can tell thee where that saying was born, of 'I fear no colors.' 10

Clo. Where, good Mistress Mary?

Mar. In the wars; and that may you be bold to say in your foolery.

Clo. Well, God give them wisdom that have it; and those that are fools, let them use their talents.

Mar. Yet you will be hanged for being so long absent; or, to be turned away, is not that as good as a hanging to you? 20

Clo. Many a good hanging prevents a bad marriage; and, for turning away, let summer bear it out.

Mar. You are resolute, then?

22. *"let summer bear it out"*; summer will make it endurable.—C. H. H.

Clo. Not so, neither; but I am resolved on two points.

Mar. That if one break, the other will hold; or, if both break, your gaskins fall.

Clo. Apt, in good faith; very apt. Well, go thy way; if Sir Toby would leave drinking, 30 thou wert as witty a piece of Eve's flesh as any in Illyria.

Mar. Peace, you rogue, no more o' that. Here comes my lady: make your excuse wisely, you were best. [*Exit.*

Clo. Wit, an 't be thy will, put me into good fooling! Those wits, that think they have thee, do very oft prove fools; and I, that am sure I lack thee, may pass for a wise man: for what says Quinapalus? 'Better a 40 witty fool than a foolish wit.'

Enter Lady Olivia with Malvolio.

God bless thee, lady.

Oli. Take the fool away.

Clo. Do you not hear, fellows? Take away the lady.

Oli. Go to, you 're a dry fool; I 'll no more of you: besides, you grow dishonest.

Clo. Two faults, madonna, that drink and good counsel will amend: for give the dry fool drink, then is the fool not dry: bid the dis- 50 honest man mend himself; if he mend, he is

26. *"Points"* were laces which fastened the hose or breeches. Thus Falstaff: "Their points broken, down fell their hose." Maria is of course punning on *points*.—H. N. H.

no longer dishonest; if he cannot, let the botcher mend him. Any thing that 's mended is but patched: virtue that transgresses is but patched with sin; and sin that amends is but patched with virtue. If that this simple syllogism will serve, so; if it will not, what remedy? As there is no true cuckold but calamity, so beauty 's a flower. The lady bade take away the fool; therefore 60
I say again, take her away.

Oli. Sir, I bade them take away you.

Clo. Misprision in the highest degree! Lady, cucullus non facit monachum; that 's as much to say as I wear not motley in my brain. Good madonna, give me leave to prove you a fool.

Oli. Can you do it?

Clo. Dexteriously, good madonna.

Oli. Make your proof. 70

Clo. I must catechize you for it, madonna: good my mouse of virtue, answer me.

Oli. Well, sir, for want of other idleness, I 'll bide your proof.

Clo. Good madonna, why mournest thou?

Oli. Good fool, for my brother's death.

Clo. I think his soul is in hell, madonna.

Oli. I know his soul is in heaven, fool.

Clo. The more fool, madonna, to mourn for your brother's soul being in heaven. Take 80
away the fool, gentlemen.

Oli. What think you of this fool, Malvolio? doth he not mend?

Mal. Yes, and shall do till the pangs of death shake him: infirmity, that decays the wise, doth ever make the better fool.

Clo. God send you, sir, a speedy infirmity, for the better increasing your folly! Sir Toby will be sworn that I am no fox; but he will not pass his word for two pence that you are no fool. 90

Oli. How say you to that, Malvolio?

Mal. I marvel your ladyship takes delight in such a barren rascal: I saw him put down the other day with an ordinary fool that has no more brain than a stone. Look you now, he 's out of his guard already; unless you laugh and minister occasion to him, he is gagged. I protest, I take these wise men, that crow so at these set kind of fools, no better than fools' zanies. 100

Oli. O, you are sick of self-love, Malvolio, and taste with a distempered appetite. To be generous, guiltless and of free disposition, is to take those things for bird-bolts that you deem cannon-bullets: there is no slander in an allowed fool, though he do nothing but rail; nor no railing in a known discreet man, though he do nothing but reprove.

Clo. Now Mercury endue thee with leasing, for thou speakest well of fools! 110

Re-enter Maria.

Mar. Madam, there is at the gate a young gentleman much desires to speak with you.

Oli. From the Count Orsino, is it?

Mar. I know not, madam: 'tis a fair young man, and well attended.

Oli. Who of my people hold him in delay?

Mar. Sir Toby, madam, your kinsman.

Oli. Fetch him off, I pray you; he speaks nothing but madman: fie on him! [*Exit Maria.*] 120 Go you, Malvolio: if it be a suit from the count, I am sick, or not at home; what you will, to dismiss it. [*Exit Malvolio.*] Now you see, sir, how your fooling grows old, and people dislike it.

Clo. Thou hast spoke for us, madonna, as if thy eldest son should be a fool; whose skull Jove cram with brains! for,—here he comes,— one of thy kin has a most weak pia mater.

Enter Sir Toby.

Oli. By mine honor, half drunk. What is he at 130 the gate, cousin?

Sir To. A gentleman.

Oli. A gentleman! what gentleman?

Sir To. 'Tis a gentleman here—a plague o' these pickle-herring! How now, sot!

Clo. Good Sir Toby!

Oli. Cousin, cousin, how have you come so early by this lethargy?

129. *"weak pia mater"*; the membrane that covers the brain.—H. N. H.

135. *"pickle-herring"*; Sir Toby attributes the enforced interruption of his speech to the pickled herrings he has eaten.—C. H. H.

"Sot" is often used by the Poet for *fool;* as in *The Merry Wives* Dr. Caius says,—"Have you make-a de *sot* of us?"—H. N. H.

Sir To. Lechery! I defy lechery. There 's one at the gate. 14

Oli. Aye, marry, what is he?

Sir To. Let him be the devil, an he will, I care not: give me faith, say I. Well, it 's all one. [*Exit*

Oli. What 's a drunken man like, fool?

Clo. Like a drowned man, a fool and a mad man: one draught above heat makes him a fool; the second mads him; and a third drowns him.

Oli. Go thou and seek the crowner, and let him sit o' my coz; for he 's in the third degree of 150 drink, he 's drowned: go look after him.

Clo. He is but mad yet, madonna; and the fool shall look to the madman. [*Exit*

Re-enter Malvolio.

Mal. Madam, yond young fellow swears he will speak with you. I told him you were sick; he takes on him to understand so much, and therefore comes to speak with you. I told him you were asleep; he seems to have a foreknowledge of that too, and therefore comes to speak with you. What is to be said to 160 him, lady? he 's fortified against any denial.

Oli. Tell him he shall not speak with me.

Mal. Has been told so; and he says, he 'll stand at your door like a sheriff's post, and be the

146. *"above heat"*; above the point at which thirst is quenched.—C. H. H.

supporter to a bench, but he 'll speak with you.

Oli. What kind o' man is he?

Mal. Why, of mankind.

Oli. What manner of man?

Mal. Of very ill manner: he 'll speak with you, will you or no. 170

Oli. Of what personage and years is he?

Mal. Not yet old enough for a man, nor young enough for a boy; as a squash is before 'tis a peascod, or a codling when 'tis almost an apple: 'tis with him in standing water, between boy and man. He is very well-favored and he speaks very shrewishly; one would think his mother's milk were scarce out of him. 180

Oli. Let him approach: call in my gentlewoman.

Mal. Gentlewoman, my lady calls. [*Exit.*

Re-enter Maria.

Oli. Give me my veil: come, throw it o'er my face.
We 'll once more hear Orsino's embassy.

Enter Viola, and Attendants.

Vio. The honorable lady of the house, which is she?

Oli. Speak to me; I shall answer for her. Your will?

175. A "*codling,*" according to Mr. Gifford, means an *involucrum* or *kell,* and was used by our old writers for that early state of vegetation, when the fruit, after shaking off the blossom, began to assume a globular and determinate shape.—H. N. H.

Vio. Most radiant, exquisite and unmatchable beauty,—I pray you, tell me if this be the lady of the house, for I never saw her: I would be loath to cast away my speech, for besides that it is excellently well penned, I have taken great pains to con it. Good beauties, let me sustain no scorn; I am very comptible, even to the least sinister usage. 190

Oli. Whence came you, sir?

Vio. I can say little more than I have studied, and that question 's out of my part. Good gentle one, give me modest assurance if you be the lady of the house, that I may proceed in my speech. 200

Oli. Are you a comedian?

Vio. No, my profound heart: and yet, by the very fangs of malice I swear, I am not that I play. Are you the lady of the house?

Oli. If I do not usurp myself, I am.

Vio. Most certain, if you are she, you do usurp yourself; for what is yours to bestow is not yours to reserve. But this is from my commission: I will on with my speech in your praise, and then show you the heart of my message. 210

Oli. Come to what is important in 't: I forgive you the praise.

Vio. Alas, I took great pains to study it, and 'tis poetical.

Oli. It is the more like to be feigned. I pray

208. *"usurp"*; counterfeit.—C. H. H.
211. *"from"*; beyond, apart from.—C. H. H.

you, keep it in. I heard you were saucy at 220
my gates, and allowed your approach rather
to wonder at you than to hear you. If you
be not mad, be gone; if you have reason, be
brief; 'tis not that time of moon with me to
make one in so skipping a dialogue.

Mar. Will you hoist sail, sir? here lies your way.

Vio. No, good swabber; I am to hull here a
little longer. Some mollification for your
giant, sweet lady. Tell me your mind: I am
a messenger. 230

Oli. Sure, you have some hideous matter to deliver, when the courtesy of it is so fearful.
Speak your office.

Vio. It alone concerns your ear. I bring no
overture of war, no taxation of homage: I
hold the olive in my hand; my words are as
full of peace as matter.

Oli. Yet you began rudely. What are you?
what would you?

Vio. The rudeness that hath appeared in me 240
have I learned from my entertainment.
What I am, and what I would, are as secret
as maiden-head; to your ears, divinity, to any
other's, profanation.

220. *"keep it in"*; keep it to yourself.—C. H. H.

229. *"giant"*; said ironically of Maria, who is elsewhere called "the youngest wren of nine."—C. H. H.

230. *"I am a messenger"*; this is usually printed thus:

"*Oli.* Tell me your mind.
Vio. I am a messenger."

We give the passage as it stands in the original; the sense being, —"I am a messenger; therefore tell me your mind that I may bear back an answer." So that the change is quite needless, though the meaning be clear enough either way.—H. H. H.

Oli. Give us the place alone: we will hear this divinity. [*Exeunt Maria and Attendants.*]
Now, sir, what is your text?

Vio. Most sweet lady,—

Oli. A comfortable doctrine, and much may be said of it. Where lies your text? 250

Vio. In Orsino's bosom.

Oli. In his bosom! In what chapter of his bosom?

Vio. To answer by the method, in the first of his heart.

Oli. O, I have read it: it is heresy. Have you no more to say?

Vio. Good madam, let me see your face.

Oli. Have you any commission from your lord to negotiate with my face? You are now 260 out of your text: but we will draw the curtain and show you the picture. Look you, sir, such a one I was this present: is 't not well done? [*Unveiling.*

Vio. Excellently done, if God did all.

Oli. 'Tis in grain, sir; 'twill endure wind and weather.

Vio. 'Tis beauty truly blent, whose red and white
Nature's own sweet and cunning hand laid on:
Lady, you are the cruel'st she alive, 270
If you will lead these graces to the grave

263. *"such a one I was this present"*; modern editions generally insert *as* before *I*, and then turn the adjective, *present*, into a verb: "such a one as I was, this presents." It is to be borne in mind that the idea of a picture is continued. So that the change is worse than useless; the meaning being,—"behold the picture of me, such as I am at the present moment."—H. N. H.

And leave the world no copy.

Oli. O, sir, I will not be so hard-hearted; I will give out divers schedules of my beauty: it shall be inventoried, and every particle and utensil labeled to my will: as, item, two lips indifferent red; item, two gray eyes, with lids to them; item, one neck, one chin, and so forth. Were you sent hither to praise me?

Vio. I see you what you are, you are too proud;
But, if you were the devil, you are fair. 281
My lord and master loves you: O, such love
Could be but recompensed, though you were crown'd
The nonpareil of beauty!

Oli. How does he love me?

Vio. With adorations, fertile tears,
With groans that thunder love, with sighs of fire.

Oli. Your lord does know my mind; I cannot love him:
Yet I suppose him virtuous, know him noble,
Of great estate, of fresh and stainless youth;
In voices well divulged, free, learn'd and valiant; 290
And in dimension and the shape of nature
A gracious person: but yet I cannot love him;
He might have took his answer long ago.

Vio. If I did love you in my master's flame,

290. *"In voices well divulged";* well reputed in the popular voice. —C. H. H.

"learned and valiant; that is, well-reputed for his knowledge in languages, which was esteemed a great accomplishment in the Poet's time.—H. N. H.

With such a suffering, such a deadly life,
In your denial I would find no sense;
I would not understand it.

Oli. Why, what would you?

Vio. Make me a willow cabin at your gate,
And call upon my soul within the house;
Write loyal cantons of contemned love 300
And sing them loud even in the dead of night;
Halloo your name to the reverberate hills,
And make the babbling gossip of the air
Cry out 'Olivia!' O, you should not rest
Between the elements of air and earth,
But you should pity me!

Oli. You might do much.
What is your parentage?

Vio. Above my fortunes, yet my state is well:
I am a gentleman.

Oli. Get you to your lord;
I cannot love him: let him send no more; 310
Unless, perchance, you come to me again,
To tell me how he takes it. Fare you well:
I thank you for your pains: spend this for me.

Vio. I am no fee'd post, lady; keep your purse:
My master, not myself, lacks recompense.
Love make his heart of flint that you shall love;
And let your fervor, like my master's, be
Placed in contempt! Farewell, fair cruelty.
[*Exit.*

Oli. 'What is your parentage?'
'Above my fortunes, yet my state is well: 320

303. *"babbling gossip of the air"*; a Shakespearean expression for *echo.*—H. N. H.

I am a gentleman.' I 'll be sworn thou art;
Thy tongue, thy face, thy limbs, actions, and spirit,
Do give thee five-fold blazon: not too fast: soft, soft!
Unless the master were the man. How now!
Even so quickly may one catch the plague?
Methinks I feel this youth's perfections
With an invisible and subtle stealth
To creep in at mine eyes. Well, let it be.
What ho, Malvolio!

Re-enter Malvolio.

Mal. Here, madam, at your service.
Oli. Run after that same peevish messenger, 330
The county's man: he left this ring behind him,
Would I or not: tell him I 'll none of it.
Desire him not to flatter with his lord,
Nor hold him up with hopes; I am not for him:
If that the youth will come this way to-morrow,
I 'll give him reasons for 't: hie thee, Malvolio.
Mal. Madam, I will. [*Exit.*
Oli. I do I know not what, and fear to find
Mine eye too great a flatterer for my mind.
Fate, show thy force: ourselves we do not owe;
What is decreed must be, and be this so. 341
[*Exit.*

339. *"Mine eye too great a flatterer";* that is, she fears that her eyes had formed so flattering an idea of the supposed youth Cesario, that she should not have strength of mind sufficient to resist the impression.—H. N. H.

ACT SECOND

Scene I

The sea-coast.

Enter Antonio and Sebastian.

Ant. Will you stay no longer? nor will you not that I go with you?

Seb. By your patience, no. My stars shine darkly over me: the malignancy of my fate might perhaps distemper yours; therefore I shall crave of you your leave that I may bear my evils alone: it were a bad recompense for your love, to lay any of them on you.

Ant. Let me yet know of you whither you are bound. 10

Seb. No, sooth, sir: my determinate voyage is mere extravagancy. But I perceive in you so excellent a touch of modesty, that you will not extort from me what I am willing to keep in; therefore it charges me in manners the rather to express myself. You must know of me then, Antonio, my name is Sebastian, which I called Roderigo. My father was that Sebastian of Messaline,

19. *"Messaline"*; possibly an error for Mitylene, as Capell conjectured.—I. G.

whom I know you have heard of. He left 20
behind him myself and a sister, both born in
an hour: if the heavens had been pleased,
would we had so ended! but you, sir, altered
that; for some hour before you took me from
the breach of the sea was my sister drowned.

Ant. Alas the day.

Seb. A lady, sir, though it was said she much
resembled me, was yet of many accounted
beautiful: but, though I could not with such
estimable wonder overfar believe that, yet 30
thus far I will boldly publish her; she bore
a mind that envy could not but call fair.
She is drowned already, sir, with salt water,
though I seem to drown her remembrance
again with more.

Ant. Pardon me, sir, your bad entertainment.

Seb. O good Antonio, forgive me your trouble.

Ant. If you will not murder me for my love,
let me be your servant.

39. *"your servant";* Mr. Knight thinks, and apparently with good reason, that in this passage reference is had to a superstition thus indicated by Sir Walter Scott in *The Pirate:* When Mordaunt has rescued Cleveland from the sea, and is trying to revive him, Bryce the peddler says to him,—"Are you mad? you, that have so long lived in Zetland, to risk the saving of a drowning man? Wot ye not, if you bring him to life again, he will be sure to do you some capital injury?" Sir Walter suggests in a note that this inhuman maxim was probably held by the islanders of the Orkneys, as an excuse for leaving all to perish alone who were shipwrecked upon their coasts, to the end that there might be nothing to hinder the plundering of their goods; which of course could not well be, if any of the owners survived. This practice, he says, continued into the eighteenth century, and "was with difficulty weeded out by the sedulous instructions of the clergy and the rigorous injunctions of the proprietors."—H. N. H.

Seb. If you will not undo what you have done, 40
that is, kill him whom you have recovered,
desire it not. Fare ye well at once: my
bosom is full of kindness, and I am yet so
near the manners of my mother, that upon
the least occasion more mine eyes will tell
tales of me. I am bound to the Count Orsino's court: farewell. [*Exit.*

Ant. The gentleness of all the gods go with thee!
I have many enemies in Orsino's court,
Else would I very shortly see thee there. 50
But, come what may, I do adore thee so,
That danger shall seem sport, and I will go.
[*Exit.*

SCENE II

A street.

Enter Viola, Malvolio following.

Mal. Were not you even now with the Countess
Olivia?

Vio. Even now, sir; on a moderate pace I have
since arrived but hither.

Mal. She returns this ring to you, sir: you
might have saved me my pains, to have taken
it away yourself. She adds, moreover, that
you should put your lord into a desperate
assurance she will none of him: and one
thing more, that you be never so hardy to 10
come again in his affairs, unless it be to re-

port your lord's taking of this. Receive it
so.

Vio. She took the ring of me: I 'll none of it.

Mal. Come, sir, you peevishly threw it to her;
and her will is, it should be so returned: if it
be worth stooping for, there it lies in your
eye; if not, be it his that finds it. [*Exit.*

Vio. I left no ring with her: what means this lady?
Fortune forbid my outside have not charm'd
her! 20
She made good view of me; indeed, so much,
That methought her eyes had lost her tongue,
For she did speak in starts distractedly.
She loves me, sure; the cunning of her passion
Invites me in this churlish messenger.
None of my lord's ring! why, he sent her none.
I am the man: if it be so, as 'tis,
Poor lady, she were better love a dream.
Disguise, I see, thou art a wickedness,
Wherein the pregnant enemy does much. 30
How easy is it for the proper-false
In women's waxen hearts to set their forms!
Alas, our frailty is the cause, not we!
For such as we are made of, such we be.

12. *"Receive it so"*; that is, understand it so.—H. N. H.

22. *"had lost her tongue"*; that is, the fixed and eager view she took of me perverted the use of her tongue, and made her talk distractedly.—H. N. H.

34. *"Such"* evidently refers to frailty in the preceding line; the sense being,—"Since we are made of frailty, we must needs be frail." The original, however, reads,—"For, such as we are made, *if* such we be"; that is, if we be frail, we are such as we are made. So that the sense seems good enough either way; which breeds no little doubt whether Malone's emendation ought to be admitted.—H. N. H.

How will this fadge? my master loves her
dearly;
And I, poor monster, fond as much on him;
And she, mistaken, seems to dote on me.
What will become of this? As I am man,
My state is desperate for my master's love;
As I am woman,—now alas the day!— 40
What thriftless sighs shall poor Olivia breathe!
O time! thou must untangle this, not I;
It is too hard a knot for me to untie! [*Exit.*

Scene III

Olivia's house.

Enter Sir Toby and Sir Andrew.

Sir To. Approach, Sir Andrew: not to be a-bed after midnight is to be up betimes; and 'diluculo surgere,' thou know'st,—

Sir And. Nay, by my troth, I know not: but I know, to be up late is to be up late.

Sir To. A false conclusion: I hate it as an unfilled can. To be up after midnight and to go to bed then, is early: so that to go to bed after midnight is to go to bed betimes. Does not our life consist of the four elements? 10

Sir And. Faith, so they say; but I think it rather consists of eating and drinking.

13. *"eating and drinking";* a ridicule of the medical theory of that time, which supposed health to consist in the just tempera-

Sir To. Thou 'rt a scholar; let us therefore eat and drink. Marian, I say! a stoup of wine!

Enter Clown.

Sir And. Here comes the fool, i' faith.

Clo. How now, my hearts! did you never see the picture of 'we three'?

Sir To. Welcome, ass. Now let 's have a catch.

Sir And. By my troth, the fool has an excellent breast. I had rather than forty shillings I had such a leg, and so sweet a breath to sing, as the fool has. In sooth, thou wast in very gracious fooling last night, when thou spokest of Pigrogromitus, of the Vapians passing the equinoctial of Queubus: 'twas very good, i' faith. I sent thee sixpence for thy leman: hadst it? 20

Clo. I did impeticos thy gratillity; for Malvolio's nose is no whipstock: my lady has a white hand, and the Myrmidons are no bottle-ale houses. 30

Sir And. Excellent! why, this is the best fooling, when all is done. Now, a song.

ment of the *four elements* in the human frame. Homer agrees with Sir Andrew:

"Strength consists in spirits and in blood,
And those are ow'd to generous wine and food."—H. N. H.

18. *"the picture of 'we three'"*; "a common sign, in which two wooden heads are exhibited with this inscription under it, *'We three loggerheads be,'* the spectator being supposed to make the third" (Malone).—I. G.

25–27. *"Pigrogromitus . . . of Queubus,"* etc. Mr. Swinburne sees in these "freaks of nomenclature" the direct influence of Rabelais (*cp. A Study of Shakespeare,* pp. 155, 156).—I. G.

Sir To. Come on; there is sixpence for you: let 's have a song.

Sir And. There 's a testril of me, too: if one knight give a—

Clo. Would you have a love-song, or a song of good life? 40

Sir. To. A love-song, a love-song.

Sir And. Aye, aye: I care not for good life.

Clo. [*Sings*]

O mistress mine, where are you roaming?
O, stay and hear; your true love 's coming,
That can sing both high and low:
Trip no further, pretty sweeting;
Journeys end in lovers meeting,
Every wise man's son doth know.

Sir And. Excellent good, i' faith.

Sir To. Good, good. 50

Clo. [*Sings*]

What is love? 'tis not hereafter;
Present mirth hath present laughter;
What 's to come is still unsure:
In delay there lies no plenty;
Then come kiss me, sweet and twenty,
Youth 's a stuff will not endure.

43. *"O mistress mine,"* etc.; "this tune is contained in both the editions of Morley's *Consort Lessons,* 1599 and 1611. It is also found in Queen Elizabeth's Virginal Book, arranged by Boyd. As it is to be found in print in 1599, it proves either that Shakespeare's *Twelfth Night* was written in or before that year, or that, in accordance with the then prevailing custom, *"O mistress mine,"* was an old song, introduced into the play" (Chappell's *Popular Music of the Olden Time*).—I. G.

55. *"Sweet-and-twenty"* appears to have been an ancient term of endearment.—H. N. H.

Sir And. A mellifluous voice, as I am true knight.

Sir To. A contagious breath.

Sir And. Very sweet and contagious, i' faith. 60

Sir To. To hear by the nose, it is dulcet in contagion. But shall we make the welkin dance indeed? shall we rouse the night-owl in a catch that will draw three souls out of one weaver? shall we do that?

Sir And. An you love me, let 's do 't: I am dog at a catch.

Clo. By 'r lady, sir, and some dogs will catch well.

Sir And. Most certain. Let our catch be, 70 'Thou knave.'

Clo. 'Hold thy peace, thou knave,' knight? I shall be constrained in 't to call thee knave, knight.

Sir And. 'Tis not the first time I have constrained one to call me knave. Begin, fool: it begins 'Hold thy peace.'

Clo. I shall never begin if I hold my peace.

Sir And. Good, i' faith. Come, begin.

[*Catch sung.*

Enter Maria.

Mar. What a caterwauling do you keep here! 80 If my lady have not called up her steward Malvolio and bid him turn you out of doors, never trust me.

Sir To. My lady 's a Cataian, we are politi-

66. *"dog at a catch"*; apt, good at.—C. H. H.

cians, Malvolio 's a Peg-a-Ramsey, and 'Three merry men be we.' Am not I consanguineous? am I not of her blood? Tillyvally. Lady! [*Sings*] 'There dwelt a man in Babylon, lady, lady!'

Clo. Beshrew me, the knight 's in admirable fooling. 90

Sir And. Aye, he does well enough if he be disposed, and so do I too: he does it with a better grace, but I do it more natural.

Sir To. [*Sings*] 'O, the twelfth day of December',—

Mar. For the love o' God, peace!

Enter Malvolio.

Mal. My masters, are you mad? or what are you? Have you no wit, manners, nor honesty, but to gabble like tinkers at this time of 100 night? Do ye make an alehouse of my lady's house, that ye squeak out your coziers' catches without any mitigation or remorse of

95. *"O, the twelfth day of December";* with Sir Toby as wine goes in music comes out, and fresh songs keep bubbling up in his memory as he waxes mellower. A similar thing occurs in *2 Henry IV,* where master Silence grows merry and musical amidst his cups in "the sweet of the night." Of the ballads referred to by Sir Toby, "O! the twelfth day of December" is entirely lost. Percy has one stanza of "There dwelt a man in Babylon," which he describes as "a poor dull performance, and very long." "Three merry men be we" seems to have been the burden of several old songs, one of which was called *"Robin Hood and the Tanner." "Peg-a-Ramsey,"* or *Peggy Ramsey,* was an old popular tune which had several ballads fitted to it. "Thou knave" was a catch which, says Sir John Hawkins, "appears to be so contrived that each of the singers calls the other knave in turn."—H. N. H.

voice? Is there no respect of place, persons, nor time in you?

Sir To. We did keep time, sir, in our catches. Sneck up!

Mal. Sir Toby, I must be round with you. My lady bade me tell you, that, though she harbors you as her kinsman, she 's nothing allied 110 to your disorders. If you can separate yourself and your misdemeanors, you are welcome to the house; if not, an it would please you to take leave of her, she is very willing to bid you farewell.

Sir To. 'Farewell, dear heart, since I must needs be gone.'

Mar. Nay, good Sir Toby.

Clo. 'His eyes do show his days are almost done.' 120

Mal. Is 't even so?

Sir To. 'But I will never die.'

Clo. Sir Toby, there you lie.

Mal. This is much credit to you.

Sir To. 'Shall I bid him go?'

Clo. 'What an if you do?'

Sir To. 'Shall I bid him go, and spare not?'

Clo. 'O no, no, no, no, you dare not.'

Sir To. Out o' tune, sir: ye lie. Art any more than a steward? Dost thou think, because 130

129. *"Out o' tune, sir: ye lie"*; Theobald proposed *"time, sir?"* which has been very generally adopted. The reading of the Folios may well stand without change. Sir Toby says to the Clown that he is out of tune and lies in declaring *"no, no, no, you dare not"* (*i. e.* dare not bid Malvolio go). Hence next words *"Art any more than a steward,"* addressed to Malvolio.—I. G.

thou art virtuous, there shall be no more cakes and ale?

Clo. Yes, by Saint Anne, and ginger shall be hot i' the mouth too.

Sir To. Thou 'rt i' the right. Go, Sir, rub your chain with crums. A stoup of wine, Marie!

Mal. Mistress Mary, if you prized my lady's favor at any thing more than contempt, you would not give means for this uncivil rule: she shall know of it, by this hand. [*Exit.* 140

Mar. Go shake your ears.

Sir And. 'Twere as good a deed as to drink when a man 's a-hungry, to challenge him the field, and then to break promise with him and make a fool of him.

Sir To. Do 't, knight: I 'll write thee a challenge; or I 'll deliver thy indignation to him by word of mouth.

Mar. Sweet Sir Toby, be patient for to-night: since the youth of the count's was to-day 150 with my lady, she is much out of quiet. For Monsieur Malvolio, let me alone with him: if I do not gull him into a nayword, and make him a common recreation, do not think I have wit enough to lie straight in my bed: I know I can do it.

Sir To. Possess us, possess us; tell us something of him.

Mar. Marry, sir, sometimes he is a kind of puritan. 160

143. *"challenge him to the field"*; challenge him to a duel.—C. H. H.

154. *"a common recreation"*; sport for all.—C. H. H.

Sir And. O, if I thought that, I 'ld beat him like a dog!

Sir To. What, for being a puritan? thy exquisite reason, dear knight?

Sir And. I have no exquisite reason for 't, but I have reason good enough.

Mar. The devil a puritan that he is, or any thing constantly, but a time-pleaser; an affectioned ass, that cons state without book and utters it by great swarths: the best per- 170 suaded of himself, so crammed, as he thinks, with excellencies, that it is his grounds of faith that all that look on him love him; and on that vice in him will my revenge find notable cause to work.

Sir To. What wilt thou do?

Mar. I will drop in his way some obscure epistles of love; wherein, by the color of his beard, the shape of his leg, the manner of his gait, the expressure of his eye, forehead, and 180 complexion, he shall find himself most feelingly personated. I can write very like my lady your niece: on a forgotten matter we can hardly make distinction of our hands.

Sir To. Excellent! I smell a device.

Sir And. I have 't in my nose too.

Sir To. He shall think, by the letters that thou wilt drop, that they come from my niece, and that she 's in love with him.

165. *"exquisite"*; subtle.—C. H. H.

169. *"cons state without book"*; gets up rules of dignified deportment.—C. H. H.

Mar. My purpose is, indeed, a horse of that 190
color.

Sir And. And your horse now would make him
an ass.

Mar. Ass, I doubt not.

Sir. And. O, 'twill be admirable!

Mar. Sport royal, I warrant you: I know my
physic will work with him. I will plant you
two, and let the fool make a third, where he
shall find the letter: observe his construction
of it. For this night, to bed, and dream on 200
the event. Farewell. [*Exit.*

Sir To. Good night, Penthesilea.

Sir And. Before me, she 's a good wench.

Sir To. She 's a beagle, true-bred, and one that
adores me: what o' that?

Sir And. I was adored once too.

Sir To. Let 's to bed, knight. Thou hadst
need send for more money.

Sir And. If I cannot recover your niece, I am a
foul way out. 210

Sir T. Send for money, knight; if thou hast her
not i' the end, call me cut.

Sir And. If I do not, never trust me, take it
how you will.

Sir To. Come, come, I 'll go burn some sack;
'tis too late to go to bed now: come, knight;
come, knight. [*Exeunt.*

Scene IV

The Duke's palace.

Enter Duke, Viola, Curio, and others.

Duke. Give me some music. Now, good morrow, friends,
Now, good Cesario, but that piece of song,
That old and antique song we heard last night:
Methought it did relieve my passion much,
More than light airs and recollected terms
Of these most brisk and giddy-paced times:
Come, but one verse.

Cur. He is not here, so please your lordship, that should sing it.

Duke. Who was it? 10

Cur. Feste, the jester, my lord; a fool that the lady Olivia's father took much delight in. He is about the house.

Duke. Seek him out, and play the tune the while.
[*Exit Curio. Music plays.*
Come hither, boy: if ever thou shalt love,
In the sweet pangs of it remember me;
For such as I am all true lovers are,
Unstaid and skittish in all motions else,
Save in the constant image of the creature 19
That is beloved. How dost thou like this tune?

Vio. It gives a very echo to the seat
Where love is throned.

18. *"skittish"*; flighty.—C. H. H.

Duke. Thou dost speak masterly:
My life upon 't, young though thou art, thine eye
Hath stay'd upon some favor that it loves:
Hath it not, boy?
Vio. A little, by your favor.
Duke. What kind of woman is 't?
Vio. Of your complexion.
Duke. She is not worth thee, then. What years, i' faith?
Vio. About your years, my lord. 29
Duke. Too old, by heaven: let still the woman take
An elder than herself; so wears she to him,
So sways she level in her husband's heart:
For, boy, however we do praise ourselves,
Our fancies are more giddy and unfirm,
More longing, wavering, sooner lost and worn,
Than women's are.
Vio. I think it well, my lord.
Duke. Then let thy love be younger than thyself,
Or thy affection cannot hold the bent;
For women are as roses, whose fair flower 39
Being once display'd, doth fall that very hour.
Vio. And so they are: alas, that they are so;
To die, even when they to perfection grow!

Re-enter Curio and Clown.

Duke. O, fellow, come, the song we had last night.
Mark it, Cesario, it is old and plain;
The spinsters and the knitters in the sun
And the free maids that weave their thread with bones

Do use to chant it: it is silly sooth,
And dallies with the innocence of love,
Like the old age.

Clo. Are you ready, sir? 50

Duke. Aye; prithee, sing. [*Music.*

SONG.

Clo. Come away, come away, death,
And in sad cypress let me be laid;
Fly away, fly away, breath;
I am slain by a fair cruel maid.
My shroud of white, stuck all with yew,
O, prepare it!
My part of death, no one so true
Did share it.

Not a flower, not a flower sweet, 60
On my black coffin let there be strown;
Not a friend, not a friend greet
My poor corpse, where my bones shall be thrown:
A thousand thousand sighs to save,
Lay me, O, where
Sad true lover never find my grave,
To weep there!

Duke. There 's for thy pains.

Clo. No pains, sir; I take pleasure in singing, sir. 70

Duke. I 'll pay thy pleasure then.

Clo. Truly, sir, and pleasure will be paid, one time or another. you will pay for pleasure

49. The *"old age"* is the *ages past,* times of simplicity.—H. N. H

Duke. Give me now leave to leave thee.

Clo. Now, the melancholy god protect thee; and the tailor make thy doublet of changeable taffeta, for thy mind is a very opal. I would have men of such constancy put to sea, that their business might be every thing and their intent every where; for that 's it 80 that always makes a good voyage of nothing. Farewell. [*Exit.*

Duke. Let all the rest give place.

[*Curio and Attendants retire.*

Once more, Cesario,
Get thee to yond same sovereign cruelty:
Tell her, my love, more noble than the world,
Prizes not quantity of dirty lands;
The parts that fortune hath bestow'd upon her,
Tell her, I hold as giddily as fortune;
But 'tis that miracle and queen of gems
That nature pranks her in attracts my soul. 90

Vio. But if she cannot love you, sir?

Duke. I cannot be so answer'd.

Vio. Sooth, but you must.
Say that some lady, as perhaps there is,
Hath for your love as great a pang of heart
As you have for Olivia: you cannot love her;
You tell her so; must she not then be answer'd?

Duke. There is no woman's sides
Can bide the beating of so strong a passion
As love doth give my heart; no woman's heart
So big, to hold so much; they lack retention.

77. *"thy mind is a very opal"*; the opal is a gem which varies its hues, as it is viewed in different lights.—H. N. H.

Alas, their love may be call'd appetite,—101
No motion of the liver, but the palate,—
That suffer surfeit, cloyment and revolt;
But mine is all as hungry as the sea,
And can digest as much: make no compare
Between that love a woman can bear me
And that I owe Olivia.

Vio. Aye, but I know,—

Duke. What dost thou know?

Vio. Too well what love women to men may owe:
In faith, they are as true of heart as we. 110
My father had a daughter loved a man,
As it might be, perhaps, were I a woman,
I should your lordship.

Duke. And what 's her history?

Vio. A blank, my lord. She never told her love,
But let concealment, like a worm i' the bud,
Feed on her damask cheek; she pined in thought
And with a green and yellow melancholy
She sat like patience on a monument,
Smiling at grief. Was not this love indeed?
We men may say more, swear more: but indeed
Our shows are more than will; for still we prove
Much in our vows, but little in our love. 122

Duke. But died thy sister of her love, my boy?

Vio. I am all the daughters of my father's house,
And all the brothers too: and yet I know not.
Sir, shall I to this lady?

Duke. Aye that 's the theme.
To her in haste; give her this jewel; say,
My love can give no place, bide no denay.

[*Exeunt.*

Scene V

Olivia's garden.

Enter Sir Toby, Sir Andrew, and Fabian.

Sir To. Come thy ways, Signior Fabian.

Fab. Nay, I 'll come: if I lose a scruple of this sport, let me be boiled to death with melancholy.

Sir To. Wouldst thou not be glad to have the niggardly rascally sheep-biter come by some notable shame?

Fab. I would exult, man: you know, he brought me out o' favor with my lady about a bear-baiting here. 10

Sir To. To anger him we 'll have the bear again; and we will fool him black and blue: shall we not, Sir Andrew?

Sir And. An we do not, it is pity of our lives.

Sir To. Here comes the little villain.

Enter Maria.

How now, my metal of India!

Mar. Get ye all three into the box-tree: Malvolio 's coming down this walk: he has been yonder i' the sun practising behavior to his own shadow this half hour: observe him, for 20 the love of mockery; for I know this letter will make a contemplative idiot of him. Close, in the name of jesting! Lie thou

6. *"come by"*; arrive at, attain to.—C. H. H.
23. *"close"*; hide yourselves.—C. H. H.

there [*throws down a letter*]; for here comes the trout that must be caught with tickling.
[*Exit.*

Enter Malvolio.

Mal. 'Tis but fortune; all is fortune. Maria once told me she did affect me: and I have heard herself come thus near, that, should she fancy, it should be one of my complexion. Besides, she uses me with a more exalted respect than any one else that follows her. What should I think on 't? 30

Sir To. Here 's an overweening rogue!

Fab. O, peace! Contemplation makes a rare turkey-cock of him: how he jets under his advanced plumes!

Sir And. 'Slight, I could so beat the rogue!

Sir To. Peace, I say.

Mal. To be Count Malvolio!

Sir To. Ah, rogue! 40

Sir And. Pistol him, pistol him.

Sir To. Peace, peace!

Mal. There is example for 't; the lady of the Strachy married the yeoman of the wardrobe.

44. *"the lady of the Strachy"*; this is one of the unsettled problems in Shakespeare. Hunter ingeniously suggested that Shakespeare ridicules, in the scene between the Clown, as Sir Topas, and Malvolio (IV, ii.), the exorcisms by Puritan ministers, in the case of a family named *Starchy* (1596–99), and that the difficult *Strachy* was a hint to the audience to expect subsequent allusion to the Starchy affair. Others suggest *"Strozzi," "Stracci," "Stratarch."* Halliwell refers to a Russian word meaning lawyer or judge. The

Sir And. Fie on him Jezebel!

Fab. O, peace! now he 's deeply in: look how imagination blows him.

Mal. Having been three months married to her, sitting in my state,— 50

Sir To. O, for a stone-bow, to hit him in the eye!

Mal. Calling my officers about me, in my branched velvet gown; having come from a day-bed, where I have left Olivia sleeping,—

Sir To. Fire and brimstone!

Fab. O, peace, peace!

Mal. And then to have the humor of state; and after a demure travel of regard, telling them 60 I know my place as I would they should do theirs, to ask for my kinsman Toby,—

Sir. To. Bolts and shackles!

Fab. O, peace, peace, peace! now, now.

Mal. Seven of my people, with an obedient start, make out for him: I frown the while; and perchance wind up my watch, or play with my—some rich jewel. Toby approaches; courtesies there to me,—

Sir To. Shall this fellow live? 70

Fab. Though our silence be drawn from us with cars, yet peace.

incident of a lady of high rank marrying her steward is the subject of Webster's *Duchess of Malfy*.—I. G.

66. *"make out for him"*; start to fetch him.—C. H. H.

69. *"courtesies"*; it is probable that this word was used to express acts of civility and reverence, by either men or women indiscriminately.—H. N. H.

Mal. I extend my hand to him thus, quenching my familiar smile with an austere regard of control,—

Sir To. And does not Toby take you a blow o' the lips then.

Mal. Saying, 'Cousin Toby, my fortunes having cast me on your niece give me this prerogative of speech,'— 80

Sir To. What, what?

Mal. 'You must amend your drunkenness.'

Sir To. Out, scab!

Fab. Nay, patience, or we break the sinews of our plot.

Mal. 'Besides, you waste the treasure of your time with a foolish knight,'—

Sir And. That 's me, I warrant you.

Mal. 'One Sir Andrew,'—

Sir And. I knew 'twas I; for many do call me fool. 90

Mal. What employment have we here?

[*Taking up the letter.*

72. *"with cars"*; so Folio 1; the later Folios, *"with cares"*; Johnson, *"with carts"*; many emendations have been proposed. Clarke defends the original reading, and compares *"A team of horse shall not pluck that from me"* (*Two Gentlemen,* III. i.). Hanmer's suggestion *"by th' ears"* has been generally adopted.—I. G.

76. *"take"*; give.—C. H. H.

89. *"'One Sir Andrew'"*; it may be worthy of remark, that the leading ideas of Malvolio, in his *humor of state,* bear a strong resemblance to those of Alnaschar in *The Arabian Nights.* Some of the expressions too are very similar. Many Arabian fictions had found their way into obscure Latin and French books, and from thence into English ones, long before any version of *The Arabian Nights* had appeared. In *The Dialogues of Creatures Moralized,* printed early in the sixteenth century, a story similar to that of Alnaschar is related.—H. N. H.

Fab. Now is the woodcock near the gin.

Sir To. O, peace! and the spirit of humors intimate reading aloud to him.

Mal. By my life, this is my lady's hand: these be her very C's, her U's, and her T's; and thus makes she her great P's. It is, in contempt of question, her hand.

Sir And. Her C's, her U's and her T's: why that? 100

Mal. [*reads*] To the unknown beloved, this, and my good wishes:—her very phrases! By your leave, wax. Soft! and the impressure her Lucrece, with which she uses to seal: 'tis my lady. To whom should this be?

Fab. This wins, him, liver and all.

Mal. [*reads*] Jove knows I love:
But who? 110
Lips, do not move;
No man must know.

'No man must know.' What follows? the numbers altered! 'No man must know:' if this should be thee, Malvolio?

Sir To. Marry, hang thee, brock!

Mal. [*reads*] I may command where I adore;
But silence, like a Lucrece knife,
With bloodless stroke my heart doth gore:
M, O, A, I, doth sway my life. 120

Fab. A fustian riddle!

105. *"her Lucrece";* her seal, bearing the figure of Lucrece.—C. H. H.

Sir To. Excellent wench, say I.

Mal. 'M, O, A, I, doth sway my life.' Nay, but first, let me see, let me see, let me see.

Fab. What dish o' poison has she dressed him!

Sir To. And with what wing the staniel checks at it!

Mal. 'I may command where I adore.' Why, she may command me: I serve her; she is my lady. Why, this is evident to any formal 130 capacity; there is no obstruction in this: and the end,—what should that alphabetical position portend? If I could make that resemble something in me,—Softly! M, O, A, I,—

Sir To. O, aye, make up that: he is now at a cold scent.

Fab. Sowter will cry upon 't for all this, though it be as rank as a fox.

Mal. M,—Malvolio; M,—why, that begins my 140 name.

Fab. Did not I say he would work it out? the cur is excellent at faults.

Mal. M,—but then there is no consonancy in the sequel; that suffers under probation: A should follow, but O does.

Fab. And O shall end, I hope.

130. *"formal capacity"*; that is, to any one *in his senses*, or whose *capacity* is not out of *form*.—H. N. H.

136. *"make up that"*; explain that.—C. H. H.

138. *"cry upon 't"*; a hunting phrase referring to the cry of the dogs when the scent is found. "He will recover it, though your 'cold' scent be—as unmistakable as a fox's.' "—C. H. H.

Sir To. Aye, or I 'll cudgel him, and make him cry O!

Mal. And then I comes behind. 150

Fab. Aye, an you had any eye behind you, you might see more detraction at your heels than fortunes before you.

Mal. M, O, A, I; this simulation is not as the former: and yet, to crush this a little, it would bow to me, for every one of these letters are in my name. Soft! here follows prose.

[*Reads*] If this fall into thy hand, revolve. In my stars I am above thee; but be not 160 afraid of greatness: some are born great, some achieve greatness, and some have greatness thrust upon 'em. Thy Fates open their hands; let thy blood and spirit embrace them; and, to inure thyself to what thou art like to be, cast thy humble slough and appear fresh. Be opposite with a kinsman, surly with servants; let thy tongue tang arguments of state; put thyself into the trick of singularity: she thus advises thee 170 that sighs for thee. Remember who commended thy yellow stockings, and wished to see thee ever cross-gartered: I say, remember. Go to, thou art made, if thou desirest to be so; if not, let me see thee a steward still, the fellow of servants, and not worthy to touch Fortune's fingers. Farewell. She that would alter services with thee,

THE FORTUNATE-UNHAPPY.

Daylight and champain discovers not more; 180
this is open. I will be proud, I will read
politic authors, I will baffle Sir Toby, I will
wash off gross acquaintance, I will be point-
devise the very man. [I do not now fool myself, to let imagination jade me; for every
reason excites to this, that my lady loves me.
She did commend my yellow stockings of
late, she did praise my leg being cross-
gartered; and in this she manifests herself to
my love, and with a kind of injunction 190
drives me to these habits of her liking. I
thank my stars I am happy. I will be
strange, stout, in yellow stockings, and
cross-gartered, even with the swiftness of
putting on. Jove and my stars be praised!
Here is yet a postscript. [*Reads*] Thou
canst not choose but know who I am. If
thou entertainest my love, let it appear in
thy smiling; thy smiles become thee well;
therefore in my presence still smile, dear my 200
sweet, I prithee.
Jove, I thank thee: I will smile; I will do
everything that thou wilt have me.] [*Exit.*

Fab. I will not give my part of this sport for a
pension of thousands to be paid from the
Sophy.

Sir To. I could marry this wench for this device,—

Sir And. So could I too.

180. *"champain"*; open country.—C. H. H.
182. *"politic"*; political.—C. H. H.

Sir To. And ask no other dowry with her but such another jest. 210

Sir And. Nor I neither.

Fab. Here comes my noble gull-catcher.

Re-enter Marie.

Sir To. Wilt thou set thy foot o' my neck?

Sir And. Or o' mine either?

Sir To. Shall I play my freedom at tray-trip, and become thy bond-slave?

Sir And. I' faith, or I either?

Sir To. Why, thou hast put him in such a dream, that when the image of it leaves him 220 he must run mad.

Mar. Nay, but say true; does it work upon him?

Sir To. Like aqua-vitæ with a midwife.

Mar. If you will then see the fruits of the sport, mark his first approach before my lady: he will come to her in yellow stockings, and 'tis a color she abhors, and cross-gartered, a fashion she detests; and he will smile upon her, which will now be so unsuitable to her disposition, being addicted to a 230 melancholy as she is, that it cannot but turn him into a notable contempt. If you will see it, follow me.

Sir To. To the gates of Tartar, thou most excellent devil of wit!

Sir And. I'll make one too. [*Exeunt.*

232. *"contempt"*; object of contempt.—C. H. H.

ACT THIRD

Scene I

Olivia's garden.

Enter Viola, and Clown with a tabor.

Vio. Save thee, friend, and thy music: dost thou live by thy tabor?

Clo. No, sir, I live by the church.

Vio. Art thou a churchman?

Clo. No such matter, sir: I do live by the church; for I do live at my house, and my house doth stand by the church.

Vio. So thou mayst say, the king lies by a beggar, if a beggar dwell near him; or, the church stands by thy tabor, if thy tabor stand by the church. 10

Clo. You have said, sir. To see this age! A sentence is but a cheveril glove to a good wit: how quickly the wrong side may be turned outward!

Vio. Nay, that 's certain; they that dally nicely with words may quickly make them wanton.

Clo. I would, therefore, my sister had had no name, sir.

4. *"churchman";* clergyman.—C. H. H.

Vio. Why, man? 20

Clo. Why, sir, her name 's a word; and to dally with that word might make my sister wanton. But indeed words are very rascals since bonds disgraced them.

Vio. Thy reason, man?

Clo. Troth, sir, I can yield you none without words; and words are grown so false, I am loath to prove reason with them.

Vio. I warrant thou art a merry fellow and carest for nothing. 30

Clo. Not so, sir, I do care for something; but in my conscience, sir, I do not care for you: if that be to care for nothing, sir, I would it would make you invisible.

Vio. Art not thou the Lady Olivia's fool?

Clo. No, indeed, sir; the Lady Olivia has no folly: she will keep no fool, sir, till she be married; and fools are as like husbands as pilchards are to herrings; the husband 's the bigger: I am indeed not her fool, but her 40 corrupter of words.

Vio. I saw thee late at the Count Orsino's.

Clo. Foolery, sir, does walk about the orb like the sun, it shines every where. I would be sorry, sir, but the fool should be as oft with your master as with my mistress: I think I saw your wisdom there.

Vio. Nay, an thou pass upon me, I 'll no more with thee. Hold, there 's expenses for thee.

24. *"bonds";* used in a double sense, (1) confinement; (2) money bonds.—C. H. H.

Clo. Now Jove, in his next commodity of hair, 50
send thee a beard!

Vio. By my troth, I 'll tell thee, I am almost sick for one; [*Aside*] though I would not have it grow on my chin. Is thy lady within?

Clo. Would not a pair of these have bred, sir?

Vio. Yes, being kept together and put to use.

Clo. I would play Lord Pandarus of Phrygia, sir, to bring a Cressida to this Troilus.

Vio. I understand you, sir; 'tis well begged. 60

Clo. The matter, I hope, is not great, sir, begging but a beggar: Cressida was a beggar. My lady is within, sir. I will construe to them whence you come; who you are and what you would are out of my welkin, I might say 'element,' but the word is overworn. [*Exit.*

Vio. This fellow is wise enough to play the fool;
And to do that well craves a kind of wit:
He must observe their mood on whom he jests,
The quality of persons, and the time, 71
And, like the haggard, check at every feather
That comes before his eye. This is a practice

50. *"commodity"*; parcel.—C. H. H.

56. *"these"*; *i. e.* these coins which Viola has given him.—I. G.

62. *"Cressida was a beggar"*; "according to the story Cressida finally became a leper and begged by the roadside."—I. G.

69. *"craves"*; requires.—C. H. H.

72. *"And, like the haggard, check at every feather"*; so the Folios; Johnson proposed *"not"* for *'and,"* and this reading has reasonably been adopted by most editors; *"to check"* is "a term in falconry, applied to a hawk when she forsakes her proper game, and follows some other of inferior kind. that crosses her in her flight"; the meaning therefore of the Folio reading would be "that he must

As full of labor as a wise man's art:
For folly that he wisely shows is fit;
But wise men, folly-fall'n, quite taint their wit.

Enter Sir Toby, and Sir Andrew.

Sir To. Save you, gentleman.
Vio. And you, sir.
Sir And. Dieu vous garde, monsieur.
Vio. Et vous aussi; votre serviteur. 80
Sir And. I hope, sir, you are; and I am yours.
Sir To. Will you encounter the house? my niece is desirous you should enter, if your trade be to her.
Vio. I am bound to your niece, sir; I mean, she is the list of my voyage.
Sir To. Taste your legs, sir; put them to motion.
Vio. My legs do better understand me, sir, than I understand what you mean by bidding me 90 taste my legs.
Sir To. I mean, to go, sir, to enter.
Vio. I will answer you with gait and entrance. But we are prevented.

Enter Olivia and Maria.

Most excellent accomplished lady, the heavens rain odors on you!

catch at every opportunity," but this does not suit the context: the wise Clown must be discriminative; hence Johnson's "*not*."—I. G.

76. "*wise men, folly-fall'n, quite taint their wit*"; Folio 1, "*wisemens folly falne*"; Hanmer and Warburton, "*wise men's folly shown*"; the text is Theobald's, and is generally adopted.—I. G.

93. "*gait*"; going.—C. H. H.

Sir And. That youth 's a rare courtier: 'Rain odors;' well.

Vio. My matter hath no voice, lady, but to your own most pregnant and vouchsafed ear. 100

Sir And. 'Odors,' 'pregnant,' and 'vouchsafed:' I 'll get 'em all three all ready.

Oli. Let the garden door be shut, and leave me to my hearing. [*Exeunt Sir Toby, Sir Andrew, and Maria.*] Give me your hand, sir.

Vio. My duty, madam, and most humble service.

Oli. What is your name?

Vio. Cesario is your servant's name, fair princess. 110

Oli. My servant, sir! 'Twas never merry world
Since lowly feigning was call'd compliment:
You 're servant to the Count Orsino, youth.

Vio. And he is yours, and his must needs be yours:
Your servant's servant is your servant, madam.

Oli. For him, I think not on him: for his thoughts,
Would they were blanks, rather than fill'd with
me!

Vio. Madam, I come to whet your gentle thoughts
On his behalf.

Oli. O, by your leave, I pray you; 120
I bade you never speak again of him:
But, would you undertake another suit,
I had rather hear you to solicit that
Than music from the spheres.

Vio. Dear lady,—

Oli. Give me leave, beseech you. I did send,

After the last enchantment you did here,
A ring in chase of you: so did I abuse
Myself, my servant and, I fear me, you:
Under your hard construction must I sit,
To force that on you, in a shameful cunning, 130
Which you knew none of yours: what might
you think?
Have you not set mine honor at the stake
And baited it with all the unmuzzled thoughts
That tyrannous heart can think? To one of
your receiving
Enough is shown; a cypress, not a bosom,
Hides my heart. So, let me hear you speak.

Vio. I pity you.

Oli. That 's a degree to love.

Vio. No, not a grize; for 'tis a vulgar proof,
That very oft we pity enemies. 139

Oli. Why, then, methinks 'tis time to smile again.
O world, how apt the poor are to be proud!
If one should be a prey, how much the better
To fall before the lion than the wolf!
[*Clock strikes.*

129. *"construction"*; sc. of my conduct.—C. H. H.

135. *"a cypress, not a bosom, Hides my heart"*; the force of these words has, it would seem, been missed; the point of the *"cypress"* is not its blackness but its transparency. *Cp. "The Ballad of Robin Hood, Scarlet and John"*:—

"Cypress over her face,
Through which her rose-like cheeks did blush
All in a comely grace."

"Bosom" must, I think, be used in this passage in the sense of "the bosom of the dress" which conceals the body. Olivia says, "you can see my heart; a thin gauze as it were hides it, not a stomacher."—I. G.

The clock upbraids me with the waste of time.
Be not afraid, good youth, I will not have you:
And yet, when wit and youth is come to harvest,
Your wife is like to reap a proper man;
There lies your way, due west.

Vio. Then westward-ho!
Grace and good disposition attend your ladyship!
You 'll nothing, madam, to my lord by me? 150

Oli. Stay:
I prithee, tell me what thou think'st of me.

Vio. That you do think you are not what you are.

Oli. If I think so, I think the same of you.

Vio. Then think you right: I am not what I am.

Oli. I would you were as I would have you be!

Vio. Would it be better, madam, than I am?
I wish it might, for now I am your fool.

Oli. O, what a deal of scorn looks beautiful
In the contempt and anger of his lip! 160
A murderous guilt shows not itself more soon
Than love that would seem hid: love's night is noon.
Cesario, by the roses of the spring,
By maidhood, honor, truth and every thing,
I love thee so, that, mauger all thy pride,
Nor wit nor reason can my passion hide.
Do not extort thy reasons from this clause,
For that I woo, thou therefore hast no cause;
But rather reason thus with reason fetter,
Love sought is good, but given unsought is better. 170

loves everything about cesario

Vio. By innocence I swear, and by my youth,

I have one heart, one bosom and one truth,
And that no woman has; nor never none
Shall mistress be of it, save I alone.
And so adieu, good madam: never more
Will I my master's tears to you deplore.

Oli. Yet come again; for thou perhaps mayst move
That heart, which now abhors, to like his love.
[*Exeunt.*

Scene II

Olivia's house.

Enter Sir Toby, Sir Andrew, and Fabian.

Sir And. No, faith, I'll not stay a jot longer.

Sir To. Thy reason, dear venom, give thy reason.

Fab. You must needs yield your reason, Sir Andrew.

Sir And. Marry, I saw your niece do more favors to the count's serving-man than ever she bestowed upon me; I saw 't i' the orchard.

Sir To. Did she see thee the while, old boy? tell me that. 10

Sir And. As plain as I see you now.

Fab. This was a great argument of love in her toward you.

Sir And. 'Slight, will you make an ass o' me?

Fab. I will prove it legitimate, sir, upon the oaths of judgment and reason.

Sir To. And they have been grand-jurymen since before Noah was a sailor.

Fab. She did show favor to the youth in your sight only to exasperate you, to awake your dormouse valor, to put fire in your heart, and brimstone in your liver. You should then have accosted her; and with some excellent jests, fire-new from the mint, you should have banged the youth into dumbness. This was looked for at your hand, and this was balked: the double gilt of this opportunity you let time wash off, and you are now sailed into the north of my lady's opinion; where you will hang like an icicle on a Dutchman's beard, unless you do redeem it by some laudable attempt either of valor or policy. 20 30

Sir And. An 't be any way, it must be with valor; for policy I hate: I had as lief be a Brownist as a politician.

Sir To. Why, then, build me thy fortunes upon the basis of valor. Challenge me the count's youth to fight with him; hurt him in eleven places: my niece shall take note of it; and assure thyself, there is no love-broker in the world can more prevail in man's commendation with woman than report of valor. 40

Fab. There is no way but this, Sir Andrew.

29–30. *"sailed into the north,"* etc.; perhaps this is a reference to the discovery of Northern Nova Zembla by the Dutchman Barenz in 1596. (*Cp.* C. H. Coote's paper on *"the new map,"* l. 90. *New Shakespeare Society Publications,* 1878.)—I. G.

Sir And. Will either of you bear me a challenge to him?

Sir To. Go, write it in a martial hand; be curst and brief; it is no matter how witty, so it be eloquent and full of invention: taunt him 50 with the license of ink: if thou thou 'st him some thrice, it shall not be amiss; and as many lies as will lie in thy sheet of paper, although the sheet were big enough for the bed of Ware in England, set 'em down: go, about it. Let there be gall enough in thy ink, though thou write with a goose-pen, no matter: about it.

Sir And. Where shall I find you?

Sir To. We 'll call thee at the cubiculo: go. 60

[*Exit Sir Andrew.*

Fab. This is a dear manakin to you, Sir Toby.

51. *"if thou thou'st him";* this has been generally thought an allusion to Coke's impudent and abusive *thouing* of Sir Walter Raleigh at his trial; but it has been ascertained that the play was acted a year and a half before that trial took place. And indeed it had been no insult to *thou* Sir Walter, unless there were some pre-existing custom or sentiment to make it so. What that custom was, may be seen by the following passage from the *Rule of St. Bridget:* "None of hyghenesse schal *thou* another in spekynge, but eche schal speke reverently to other, the younger namely to the elder." One of the authors of *Guesses at Truth* has a very learned and ingenious essay on the subject, wherein he quotes the following from a book published in 1661, by George Fox the Quaker: "For this *thou* and *thee* was a sore cut to proud flesh, and them that sought self-honour; who, though they would say it to God and Christ, would not endure to have it said to themselves. So that we were often beaten and abused, and sometimes in danger of our lives, for using those words to some proud men, who would say,—*What, you ill-bred clown, do you* thou *me!*"—H. N. H.

56. *"gall";* Ox gall was one of the regular constituents of Elizabethan ink, as is shown by contemporary receipts.—C. H. H.

61. *"manakin";* contemptuous diminutive of "man."—C. H. H.

Sir To. I have been dear to him, lad, some two thousand strong, or so.

Fab. We shall have a rare letter from him: but you 'll not deliver 't?

Sir To. Never trust me, then; and by all means stir on the youth to an answer. I think oxen and wainropes cannot hale them together. For Andrew, if he were opened, and you find so much blood in his liver as 70 will clog the foot of a flea, I 'll eat the rest of the anatomy.

Fab. And his opposite, the youth, bears in his visage no great presage of cruelty.

Enter Maria.

Sir To. Look, where the youngest wren of nine comes.

Mar. If you desire the spleen, and will laugh yourselves into stitches, follow me. Yond gull Malvolio is turned heathen, a very renegado; for there is no Christian, that 80 means to be saved by believing rightly, can ever believe such impossible passages of grossness. He 'e in yellow stockings.

Sir To. And cross-gartered?

Mar. Most villanously; like a pedant that keeps a school i' the church. I have dogged him, like his murderer. He does obey every point of the letter that I dropped to betray

75. "*youngest wren of nine*"; Folio, "*mine,*" emended by Theobald. The wren is said to lay nine or ten eggs at a time, and the last hatched nestling is usually the smallest of the whole brood.—I. G.

him: he does smile his face into more lines than is in the new map with the augmentation of the Indies: you have not seen such thing as 'tis. I can hardly forbear hurling things at him. I know my lady will strike him: if she do, he 'll smile and tak 't for a great favor. 90

Sir. To. Come, bring us, bring us where he is.

[*Exeunt.*

Scene III

A street.

Enter Sebastian and Antonio.

Seb. I would not by my will have troubled you;
But, since you make your pleasure of your pains,
I will no further chide you.

Ant. I could not stay behind you; my desire,
More sharp than filed steel, did spur me forth;
And not all love to see you, though so much
As might have drawn one to a longer voyage,

90. *"the new map with the augmentation of the Indies"*; no doubt reference to the map which Hallam, in his *Literature of Europe,* calls "the best map of the 16th century"; it is found in the first edition of Hakluyt's *Voyages* (1589), but as it records discoveries made at least seven years later, it was in all probability a separate map, well known at the time, and made so as to be inserted in Hakluyt: the author was probably Mr. Emmerie Mollineux, who was also the first Englishman to make a terrestrial globe. It is noteworthy that the map shows a marked development of the geography of India proper, etc. (*Cp. Transactions of New Shakespeare Society,* 1877–79.)—I. G.

But jealousy what might befall your travel,
Being skilless in these parts; which to a stranger,
Unguided and unfriended, often prove 10
Rough and unhospitable: my willing love,
The rather by these arguments of fear,
Set forth in your pursuit.

Seb. My kind Antonio,
I can no other answer make but thanks,
And thanks; and ever......oft good turns
Are shuffled off with such uncurrent pay:
But, were my worth as is my conscience firm,
You should find better dealing. What 's to do?
Shall we go see the reliques of this town?

Ant. To-morrow, sir: best first go see your lodging. 20

Seb. I am not weary, and 'tis long to night:
I pray you, let us satisfy our eyes
With the memorials and the things of fame
That do renown this city.

Ant. Would you 'ld pardon me;
I do not without danger walk these streets:
Once, in a sea-fight, 'gainst the count his galleys
I did some service; of such note indeed,

15. *"And thanks; and ever . . . oft good turns."* The Cambridge editors hold that some word has dropped out between *"ever"* and *"oft."* Many emendations have been proposed, perhaps the simplest reading is that of the Old spelling Shakespeare:—

"And thanks; and, ever oft, good turns . . ."

"ever oft" in the sense of "with perpetual frequency." Theobald proposed:—

"And thanks, and ever thanks; and oft good turns."—I. G.

16. *"uncurrent"*; out of date, worthless.—C. H. H.

That were I ta'en here it would scarce be answer'd.

Seb. Belike you slew great number of his people.

Ant. The offense is not of such a bloody nature; 30
Albeit the quality of the time and quarrel
Might well have given us bloody argument.
It might have since been answer'd in repaying
What we took from them; which, for traffic's sake,
Most of our city did: only myself stood out;
For which, if I be lapsed in this place,
I shall pay dear.

Seb. Do not then walk too open.

Ant. It doth not fit me. Hold, sir, here 's my purse.
In the south suburbs, at the Elephant,
Is best to lodge: I will bespeak our diet, 40
Whiles you beguile the time and feed your knowledge
With viewing of the town: there shall you have me.

Seb. Why I your purse?

Ant. Haply your eye shall light upon some toy
You have desire to purchase; and your store,
I think, is not for idle markets, sir.

Seb. I 'll be your purse-bearer and leave you
For an hour.

Ant. To the Elephant.

Seb. I do remember. [*Exeunt.*

Scene IV

Olivia's garden.

Enter Olivia and Maria.

Oli. I have sent after him: he says he 'll come;
How shall I feast him? what bestow of him?
For youth is bought more oft than begg'd or borrow'd.
I speak too loud.
Where is Malvolio? he is sad and civil,
And suits well for a servant with my fortunes:
Where is Malvolio?

Mar. He 's coming, madam; but in very strange manner. He is, sure, possessed, madam.

Oli. Why, what 's the matter? does he rave? 10

Mar. No, madam, he does nothing but smile: your ladyship were best to have some guard about you, if he come; for, sure, the man is tainted in 's wits.

Oli. Go call him hither. [*Exit Maria.*] I am as mad as he,
If sad and merry madness equal be.

Re-enter Maria, with Malvolio.

How now, Malvolio!

Mal. Sweet lady, ho, ho.

Oli. Smilest thou?
I sent for thee upon a sad occasion. 20

2. *"bestow of"*; bestow on.—C. H. H.

Mal. Sad, lady? I could be sad: this does make some obstruction in the blood, this cross-gartering; but what of that? if it please the eye of one, it is with me as the very true sonnet is, 'Please one, and please all.'

Oli. Why, how dost thou, man? what is the matter with thee?

Mal. Not black in my mind, though yellow in my legs. It did come to his hands, and commands shall be executed: I think we do know the sweet Roman hand. 30

Oli. Wilt thou go to bed, Malvolio?

Mal. To bed! aye, sweet-heart, and I 'll come to thee.

Oli. God comfort thee! Why dost thou smile so and kiss thy hand so oft?

Mar. How do you, Malvolio?

Mal. At your request! yes; nightingales answer daws.

Mar. Why appear you with this ridiculous boldness before my lady? 40

Mal. 'Be not afraid of greatness:' 'twas well writ.

Oli. What meanest thou by that, Malvolio?

Mal. 'Some are born great,'—

Oli. Ha!

Mal. 'Some achieve greatness,'—

Oli. What sayest thou?

Mal. 'And some have greatness thrust upon them.' 50

Oli. Heaven restore thee!

Mal. 'Remember who commended thy yellow stockings,'—

Oli. Thy yellow stockings!

Mal. 'And wished to see thee cross-gartered.'

Oli. Cross-gartered!

Mal. 'Go to, thou art made, if thou desirest to be so;'—

Oli. Am I made?

Mal. 'If not, let me see thee a servant still.' 60

Oli. Why, this is very midsummer madness.

Enter Servant.

Ser. Madam, the young gentleman of the Count Orsino's is returned: I could hardly entreat him back: he attends your ladyship's pleasure.

Oli. I 'll come to him. [*Exit Servant.*] Good Maria, let this fellow be looked to. Where 's my cousin Toby? Let some of my people have a special care of him: I would not have him miscarry for the half of 70 my dowry.

[*Exeunt Olivia and Maria.*

Mal. O, ho! do you come near me now? no worse man than Sir Toby to look to me! This concurs directly with the letter: she sends him on purpose, that I may appear stubborn to him; for she incites me to that in the letter. 'Cast thy humble slough,' says

61. *"midsummer madness"*; "'Tis midsummer moon with you," was a proverbial phrase, signifying you are mad. It was an ancient opinion that hot weather affected the brain.—H. N. H.

she; 'be opposite with a kinsman, surly with
servants; let thy tongue tang with arguments of state; put thyself into the trick of 80
singularity;' and consequently sets down the
manner how; as, a sad face, a reverend car-
riage, a slow tongue, in the habit of some
sir of note, and so forth. I have limed her;
but it is Jove's doing, and Jove make me
thankful! And when she went away now,
'Let this fellow be looked to:' fellow! not
Malvolio, nor after my degree, but fellow.
Why, every thing adheres together, that no
dram of a scruple, no scruple of a scruple, 90
no obstacle, no incredulous or unsafe circumstance—What can be said? Nothing
that can be can come between me and the
full prospect of my hopes. Well, Jove,
not I, is the doer of this, and he is to be
thanked.

Re-enter Maria, with Sir Toby and Fabian.

Sir. To. Which way is he, in the name of sanctity? If all the devils of hell be drawn in
little, and Legion himself possessed him,
yet I 'll speak to him. 100

Fab. Here he is, here he is. How is 't with you,
sir? how is 't with you, man?

Mal. Go off; I discard you: let me enjoy my
private: go off.

Mar. Lo, how hollow the fiend speaks within
him! did not I tell you? Sir Toby, my lady
prays you to have a care of him.

Mal. Ah, ha! does she so?

Sir. To. Go to, go to; peace, peace; we must deal gently with him; let me alone. How 110 do you, Malvolio? how is 't with you? What, man! defy the devil: consider, he 's an enemy to mankind.

Mal. Do you know what you say?

Mar. La you, an you speak ill of the devil, how he takes it at heart! Pray God, he be not bewitched!

Fab. Carry his water to the wise woman.

Mar. Marry, and it shall be done to-morrow morning, if I live. My lady would not lose 120 him for more than I 'll say.

Mal. How now, mistress!

Mar. O Lord!

Sir. To. Prithee, hold thy peace; this is not the way: do you not see you move him? let me alone with him.

Fab. No way but gentleness; gently, gently: the fiend is rough, and will not be roughly used.

Sir. To. Why, how now, my bawcock! how 130 dost thou, chuck?

Mal. Sir!

Sir To. Aye, Biddy, come with me. What, man! 'tis not for gravity to play at cherry-pit with Satan: hang him, foul collier!

Mar. Get him to say his prayers, good Sir Toby, get him to pray.

Mal. My prayers, minx!

Mar. No, I warrant you, he will not hear of godliness. 140

Mal. Go, hang yourselves all! you are idle shallow things: I am not of your element: you shall know more hereafter. [*Exit.*

Sir To. Is 't possible?

Fab. If this were played upon a stage now, I could condemn it as an improbable fiction.

Sir To. His very genius hath taken the infection of the device, man.

Mar. Nay, pursue him now, lest the device take air and taint. 150

Fab. Why, we shall make him mad indeed.

Mar. The house will be the quieter.

Sir To. Come, we 'll have him in a dark room and bound. My niece is already in the belief that he 's mad: we may carry it thus, for our pleasure and his penance, till our very pastime, tired out of breath, prompt us to have mercy on him: at which time we will bring the device to the bar and crown thee for a finder of madmen. But see, but see. 160

Enter Sir Andrew.

Fab. More matter for a May morning.

Sir And. Here 's the challenge, read it: I warrant there 's vinegar and pepper in 't.

Fab. Is 't so saucy?

Sir And. Aye, is 't, I warrant him: do but read.

159. *"the bar"*; the law courts.—C. H. H.

161. *"matter for May morning"*; it was usual on the First of May to exhibit metrical interludes of the comic kind as well as other sports, such as the Morris Dance.—H. N. H.

Sir To. Give me. [*Reads*] Youth, whatsoever thou art, thou art but a scurvy fellow.

Fab. Good, and valiant.

Sir To. [*reads*] Wonder not, nor admire not in thy mind, why I do call thee so, for I will show thee no reason for 't. 170

Fab. A good note; that keeps you from the blow of the law.

Sir To. [*reads*] Thou comest to the lady Olivia, and in my sight she uses thee kindly: but thou liest in thy throat; that is not the matter I challenge thee for.

Fab. Very brief, and to exceeding good sense —less

Sir To. [*reads*] I will waylay thee going home; where if it be thy chance to kill me,— 180

Fab. Good.

Sir To. [*reads*] Thou killest me like a rogue and a villain.

Fab. Still you keep o' the windy side of the law: good.

Sir To. [*reads*] Fare thee well; and God have mercy upon one of our souls! He may have mercy upon mine; but my hope is better, and so look to thyself. Thy friend, as thou usest him, and thy sworn enemy, ANDREW AGUECHEEK. If this letter move him not, his legs cannot: I 'll give 't him. 190

Mar. You may have very fit occasion for 't: he is now in some commerce with my lady, and will by and by depart.

Sir To. Go, Sir Andrew; scout me for him at

the corner of the orchard like a bum-baily:
so soon as ever thou seest him, draw; and,
as thou drawest, swear horrible; for it comes 200
to pass oft that a terrible oath, with a swaggering
accent sharply twanged off, gives
manhood more approbation than ever proof
itself would have earned him. Away!

Sir And. Nay, let me alone for swearing. [*Exit.*

Sir To. Now will not I deliver his letter: for
the behavior of the young gentleman gives
him out to be of good capacity and breeding;
his employment between his lord and my
niece confirms no less: therefore this letter, 210
being so excellently ignorant, will breed no
terror in the youth: he will find it comes
from a clodpole. But, sir, I will deliver his
challenge by word of mouth; set upon
Aguecheek a notable report of valor; and
drive the gentleman, as I know his youth
will aptly receive it, into a most hideous opinion
of his rage, skill, fury and impetuosity.
This will so fright them both, that they will
kill one another by the look, like cockatrices. 220

Re-enter Olivia, with Viola.

Fab. Here he comes with your niece: give them
way till he take leave, and presently after
him.

Sir To. I will meditate the while upon some
horrid message for a challenge.

[*Exeunt Sir Toby, Fabian, and Maria.*

Oli. I have said too much unto a heart of stone,

And laid mine honor too unchary out:
There 's something in me that reproves my fault;
But such a headstrong potent fault it is,
That it but mocks reproof. 230

Vio. With the same 'havior that your passion bears
Goes on my master's grief.

Oli. Here, wear this jewel for me, 'tis my picture;
Refuse it not; it hath no tongue to vex you;
And I beseech you come again to-morrow.
What shall you ask of me that I 'll deny,
That honor saved may upon asking give?

Vio. Nothing but this;—your true love for my master.

Oli. How with mine honor may I give him that
Which I have given to you?

Vio. I will acquit you. 240

Oli. Well, come again to-morrow: fare thee well:
A fiend like thee might bear my soul to hell.
[*Exit.*

Re-enter Sir Toby and Fabian.

Sir To. Gentleman, God save thee.

Vio. And you, sir.

Sir To. That defense thou hast, betake thee to 't: of what nature the wrongs are thou hast done him, I know not; but thy intercepter, full of despite, bloody as the hunter, attends thee at the orchard-end: dismount thy tuck, be yare in thy preparation, for thy 250 assailant is quick, skillful and deadly.

Vio. You mistake, sir; I am sure no man hath

any quarrel to me: my remembrance is very free and clear from any image of offense done to any man.

Sir To. You 'll find it otherwise, I assure you: therefore, if you hold your life at any price, betake you to your guard; for your opposite hath in him what youth, strength, skill and wrath can furnish man withal. 260

Vio. I pray you, sir, what is he?

Sir To. He is knight, dubbed with unhatched rapier and on carpet consideration; but he is a devil in private brawl: souls and bodies hath he divorced three; and his incensement at this moment is so implacable, that satisfaction can be none but by pangs of deaths and sepulcher. Hob, nob, is his word; give 't or take 't.

Vio. I will return again into the house and de- 270 sire some conduct of the lady. I am no fighter. I have heard of some kind of men that put quarrels purposely on others, to taste their valor: belike this is a man of that quirk.

Sir To. Sir, no; his indignation derives itself out of a very competent injury: therefore, get you on and give him his desire. Back you shall not to the house, unless you undertake that with me which with as much safety 280 you might answer him: therefore, on, or strip your sword stark naked; for meddle

277. *"competent injury"*; sufficient insult.—C. H. H.

you must, that 's certain, or foreswear to wear iron about you.

Vio. This is as uncivil as strange. I beseech you, do me this courteous office, as to know of the knight what my offense to him is: it is something of my negligence, nothing of my purpose.

Sir To. I will do so. Signior Fabian, stay you by this gentleman till my return. [*Exit.* 290

Vio. Pray you, sir, do you know of this matter?

Fab. I know the knight is incensed against you, even to a mortal arbitrement; but nothing of the circumstance more.

Vio. I beseech you, what manner of man is he?

Fab. Nothing of that wonderful promise, to read him by his form, as you are like to find him in the proof of his valor. He is, indeed, sir, the most skillful, bloody and fatal opposite that you could possibly have found in any part of Illyria. Will you walk towards him? I will make your peace with him if I can. 300

Vio. I shall be much bound to you for 't: I am one that had rather go with sir priest than sir knight: I care not who knows so much of my mettle. [*Exeunt.*

Re-enter Sir Toby, with Sir Andrew.

Sir To. Why, man, he 's a very devil; I have not seen such a firago. I had a pass with him, rapier, scabbard and all, and he gives me the stuck in with such a mortal motion, 310 that it is inevitable; and on the answer, he pays you as surely as your feet hit the ground they step on. They say he has been fencer to the Sophy.

Sir And. Pox on 't, I 'll not meddle with him.

Sir To. Aye, but he will not now be pacified: Fabian can scarce hold him yonder.

Sir And. Plague on 't, an I thought he had 320 been valiant and so cunning in fence, I 'ld have seen him damned ere I 'ld have challenged him. Let him let the matter slip, and I 'll give him my horse, gray Capilet.

Sir To. I 'll make the motion: stand here, make a good show on 't: this shall end without the perdition of souls. [*Aside*] Marry, I 'll ride your horse as well as I ride you.

Re-enter Fabian and Viola.

[*To Fab.*] I have his horse to take up the quarrel: I have persuaded him the youth 's a 330 devil.

Fab. He is as horribly conceited of him; and pants and looks pale, as if a bear were at his heels.

Sir To. [*To Vio.*] There 's no remedy, sir; he will fight with you for 's oath sake: marry, he hath better bethought him of his quarrel, and he finds that now scarce to be worth talking of: therefore draw, for the support-

325. *"motion"*; proposition.—C. H. H.

332. *"He is . . . of him"*; he has just as terrible an idea of him.—C. H. H.

ance of his vow; he protests he will not hurt 340
you.

Vio. [*aside*] Pray God defend me! A little
thing would make me tell them how much I
lack of a man.

Fab. Give ground, if you see him furious.

Sir To. Come, Sir Andrew, there 's no remedy;
the gentleman will, for his honor's sake,
have one bout with you; he cannot by the
duello avoid it: but he has promised me, as he
is a gentleman and a soldier, he will not hurt 350
you. Come on; to 't.

Sir And. Pray God, he keep his oath!

Vio. I do assure you, 'tis against my will.
[*They draw.*

Enter Antonio.

Ant. Put up your sword. If this young gentle-
man
Have done offense, I take the fault on me:
If you offend him, I for him defy you.

Sir To. You, sir! why, what are you?

Ant. One, sir, that for his love dares yet do more
Than you have heard him brag to you he will.

Sir To. Nay, if you be an undertaker, I am for 360
you. [*They draw.*

Enter Officers.

Fab. O good Sir Toby, hold! here come the
officers.

360. *"an undertaker"*; that is, one who takes up or *undertakes* the quarrel of another.—H. N. H.

Sir To. I 'll be with you anon.

Vio. Pray, sir, put your sword up, if you please.

Sir And. Marry, will I, sir; and, for that I promised you, I 'll be as good as my word: he will bear you easily and reins well.

First Off. This is the man; do thy office. 370

Sec. Off. Antonio, I arrest thee at the suit of Count Orsino.

Ant. You do mistake me, sir.

First Off. No, sir, no jot; I know your favor well,
Though now you have no sea-cap on your head.
Take him away: he knows I know him well.

Ant. I must obey. [*To Vio.*] This comes with seeking you:
But there 's no remedy; I shall answer it.
What will you do, now my necessity
Makes me to ask you for my purse? It grieves me 380
Much more for what I cannot do for you
Than what befalls myself. You stand amazed;
But be of comfort.

Sec. Off. Come, sir, away.

Ant. I must entreat of you some of that money.

Vio. What money, sir?
For the fair kindness you have show'd me here,
And, part, being prompted by your present trouble,
Out of my lean and low ability
I'll lend you something: my having is not much;

I 'll make division of my present with you: 390
Hold, there 's half my coffer.

Ant. Will you deny me now?
Is 't possible that my deserts to you
Can lack persuasion? Do not tempt my misery,
Lest that it make me so unsound a man
As to upbraid you with those kindnesses
That I have done for you.

Vio. I know of none;
Nor know I you by voice or any feature:
I hate ingratitude more in a man
Than lying vainness, babbling drunkenness,
Or any taint of vice whose strong corruption 400
Inhabits our frail blood.

Shakes- value

Ant. O heavens themselves!

Sec. Off. Come, sir, I pray you, go.

Ant. Let me speak a little. This youth that you see here
I snatch'd one half out of the jaws of death;
Relieved him with such sanctity of love;
And to his image, which methought did promise
Most venerable worth, did I devotion.

First Off. What 's that to us? The time goes by: away!

Ant. But O how vile an idol proves this god!
Thou hast, Sebastian, done good feature shame.
In nature there 's no blemish but the mind; 411
None can be call'd deform'd but the unkind:

391. *"coffer"*; treasure, purse.—C. H. H.
392. *"my deserts to you"*; what I deserve at your hands.—C. H. H.

Virtue is beauty; but the beauteous evil
Are empty trunks, o'erflourish'd by the devil.

First Off. The man grows mad: away with him!
Come, come, sir.

Ant. Lead me on. [*Exit with Officers.*

Vio. Methinks his words do from such passion fly,
That he believes himself: so do not I.
Prove true, imagination, O prove true,
That I, dear brother, be now ta'en for you!

Sir To. Come hither, knight; come hither, 421
Fabian: we'll whisper o'er a couplet or two
of most sage saws.

Vio. He named Sebastian: I my brother know
Yet living in my glass; even such and so
In favor was my brother, and he went
Still in this fashion, color, ornament,
For him I imitate: O, if it prove,
Tempests are kind and salt waves fresh in love!
[*Exit.*

Sir To. A very dishonest paltry boy, and more 430
a coward than a hare: his dishonesty appears
in leaving his friend here in necessity and
denying him; and for his cowardship, ask
Fabian.

Fab. A coward, a most devout coward, religious in it.

414. *"o'erflourished";* trunks, being then part of the furniture of apartments, were ornamented with scroll work or *flourished* devices. —H. N. H.

418. *"so do not I";* that is, I do not yet believe myself, when from this accident I gather hope of my brother's life.—H. N. H.

425. *"Yet living in my glass";* his resemblance *survives* in the reflection of my own figure.—H. N. H.

427. *"still";* ever.—C. H. H.

Sir And. 'Slid, I 'll after him again and beat him.

Sir To. Do; cuff him soundly, but never draw thy sword. 440

Sir And. An I do not,— [*Exit.*

Fab. Come, let 's see the event.

Sir To. I dare lay any money 'twill be nothing yet. [*Exeunt.*

ACT FOURTH

Scene I

Before Olivia's house.

Enter Sebastian and Clown.

Clo. Will you make me believe that I am not sent for you?

Seb. Go to, go to, thou art a foolish fellow: Let me be clear of thee.

Clo. Well held out, i' faith! No, I do not know you; nor I am not sent to you by my lady, to bid you come speak with her; nor your name is not Master Cesario; nor this is not my nose neither. Nothing that is so is so. 10

Seb. I prithee, vent thy folly somewhere else: Thou know'st not me.

Clo. Vent my folly! he has heard that word of some great man and now applies it to a fool. Vent my folly! I am afraid this great lub-

15, 16. *"I am afraid this great lubber, the world, will prove a cockney";* so the Folios; the lines evidently mean "I am afraid affectation and foppery will overspread the world" (Johnson); it has been proposed to change *"world"* into *"word"* (*i. e.* with reference to "vent"): others read *"this great lubberly world";* Knight explains that the words are spoken aside, and mean, "I am afraid the world will prove this great lubber (Sebastian) a cockney." This seems very strained, and probably the simplest reading of the passage is the best.—I. G.

ber, the world, will prove a cockney. I prithee now, ungird thy strangeness and tell me what I shall vent to my lady: shall I vent to her that thou art coming?

Seb. I prithee, foolish Greek, depart from me: 20
There 's money for thee: if you tarry longer,
I shall give worse payment.

Clo. By my troth, thou hast an open hand. These wise men that give fools money get themselves a good report—after fourteen years' purchase.

Enter Sir Andrew, Sir Toby, and Fabian.

Sir And. Now, sir, have I met you again? there 's for you.

Seb. Why, there 's for thee, and there, and there.
Are all the people mad? 30

Sir To. Hold, sir, or I 'll throw your dagger o'er the house.

Clo. This will I tell my lady straight: I would not be in some of your coats for two pence.

[*Exit.*

Sir To. Come on, sir; hold.

Sir And. Nay, let him alone: I 'll go another way to work with him; I 'll have an action of battery against him, if there be any law in Illyria: though I struck him first, yet it 's no matter for that. 40

Seb. Let go thy hand.

Sir To. Come, sir, I will not let you go. Come, my young soldier, put up your iron: you are well fleshed; come on.

Seb. I will be free from thee. What wouldst thou now?
If thou darest tempt me further, draw thy sword.

Sir To. What, what? Nay, then I must have an ounce or two of this malapert blood from you.

Enter Olivia.

Oli. Hold, Toby; on thy life, I charge thee, hold!

Sir To. Madam! 51

Oli. Will it be ever thus? Ungracious wretch,
Fit for the mountains and the barbarous caves,
Where manners ne'er were preach'd! out of my sight!
Be not offended, dear Cesario.
Rudesby, be gone!

[*Exeunt Sir Toby, Sir Andrew, and Fabian.*

I prithee, gentle friend,
Let thy fair wisdom, not thy passion, sway
In this uncivil and unjust extent
Against thy peace. Go with me to my house;
And hear thou there how many fruitless pranks
This ruffian hath botch'd up, that thou thereby 61
Mayst smile at this: thou shalt not choose but go:
Do not deny. Beshrew his soul for me,
He started one poor heart of mine in thee.

61. *"botch'd up"*; brought about.—C. H. H.

64. *"one poor heart of mine"*; an equivoque is here intended between *hart* and *heart,* which were formerly written alike.—H. N. H.

Seb. What relish is in this? how runs the stream?
Or I am mad, or else this is a dream:
Let fancy still my sense in Lethe steep;
If it be thus to dream, still let me sleep!

Oli. Nay, come, I prithee: would thou 'ldst be ruled by me! 69

Seb. Madam, I will.

Oli. O, say so, and so be! [*Exeunt.*

Scene II

Olivia's house.

Enter Maria and Clown.

Mar. Nay, I prithee, put on this gown and this beard; make him believe thou art Sir Topas the curate: do it quickly; I 'll call Sir Toby the whilst. [*Exit.*

Clo. Well, I 'll put it on, and I will dissemble myself in 't; and I would I were the first that ever dissembled in such a gown. I am not tall enough to become the function well, nor lean enough to be thought a good student; but to be said an honest man and a 10 good housekeeper goes as fairly as to say a careful man and a great scholar. The competitors enter.

70. *"and so be!"; sc.* ruled by me.—C. H. H.
4. *"the whilst";* meanwhile.—C. H. H.
8. *"I am not tall enough";* the modern editors have changed this to *fat* without any apparent reason; *tall* being sometimes used in the sense of *lusty,* and thus making a good antithesis to *lean.*—H. N. H.

Enter Sir Toby and Maria.

Sir To. Jove bless thee, master Parson.

Clo. Bonos dies, Sir Toby: for, as the old hermit of Prague, that never saw pen and ink, very wittily said to a niece of King Gorboduc, 'That that is is;' so I, being master Parson, am master Parson; for, what is 'that' but 'that,' and 'is' but 'is'? 20

Sir To. To him, Sir Topas.

Clo. What, ho, I say! peace in this prison!

Sir To. The knave counterfeits well; a good knave.

Mal. [*within*] Who calls there?

Clo. Sir Topas the curate, who comes to visit Malvolio the lunatic.

Mal. Sir Topas, Sir Topas, good Sir Topas, go to my lady.

Clo. Out, hyperbolical fiend! how vexest thou 30 this man! talkest thou nothing but of ladies?

Sir To. Well said, master Parson.

Mal. Sir Topas, never was man thus wronged: good Sir Topas, do not think I am mad: they have laid me here in hideous darkness.

Clo. Fie, thou dishonest Satan! I call thee by the most modest terms; for I am one of those

16. *"the old hermit of Prague";* Douce points out that the allusion is "not to the celebrated heresiarch, Jerome of Prague, but another of that name, born likewise at Prague, and called the *hermit* of Camaldoli in Tuscany."—I. G.

18. *"Gorboduc";* a legendary British king, the subject of the earliest English tragedy.—C. H. H.

20. *"and 'is' but 'is'";* a humorous banter upon the language of the schools.—H. N. H.

gentle ones that will use the devil himself with courtesy: sayest thou that house is dark? 40

Mal. As hell, Sir Topas.

Clo. Why, it hath bay windows transparent as barricadoes, and the clearstories toward the south north are as lustrous as ebony; and yet complainest thou of obstruction?

Mal. I am not mad, Sir Topas: I say to you, this house is dark.

Clo. Madman, thou errest: I say, there is no darkness but ignorance; in which thou art more puzzled than the Egyptians in their fog. 50

Mal. I say, this house is as dark as ignorance, though ignorance were as dark as hell; and I say, there was never man thus abused. I am no more mad than you are: make the trial of it in any constant question.

Clo. What is the opinion of Pythagoras concerning wild fowl?

Mal. That the soul of our grandam might haply inhabit a bird. 60

Clo. What thinkest thou of his opinion?

42. *"bay windows"* were large projecting windows, properly so called because they occupied a whole *bay* or space between two cross beams in a building. Minshew says a bay-window is so called "because it is builded in manner of a *bay* or road for ships, that is, round."—H. N. H.

43. *"clearstories"*; Folio 1, *"cleere stores"*; Folio 2, *"cleare stones"*; the reading adopted is Blakeway's conjecture in Boswell: *"clere-story"* is the name given to the windows above the arches of the nave of a Gothic church.—I. G.

50. *"Egyptians in their fog"*; a reference to the ninth plague, *Exodus* x. 21, 22.—C. H. H.

Mal. I think nobly of the soul, and no way approve his opinion.

Clo. Fare thee well. Remain thou still in darkness: thou shalt hold the opinion of Pythagoras ere I will allow of thy wits; and fear to kill a woodcock, lest thou dispossess the soul of thy grandam. Fare thee well.

Mal. Sir Topas, Sir Topas!

Sir To. My most exquisite Sir Topas! 70

Clo. Nay, I am for all waters.

Mar. Thou mightst have done this without thy beard and gown: he sees thee not.

Sir To. To him in thine own voice, and bring me word how thou findest him: I would we were well rid of this knavery. If he may be conveniently delivered, I would he were; for I am now so far in offense with my niece, that I cannot pursue with any safety this sport to the upshot. Come by and by to 80 my chamber. [*Exeunt Sir Toby and Maria.*

Clo. [*Singing*] Hey, Robin, jolly Robin,
Tell me how thy lady does.

Mal. Fool,—

Clo. My lady is unkind, perdy.

Mal. Fool,—

Clo. Alas, why is she so?

Mal. Fool, I say,—

Clo. She loves another—Who calls, ha?

Mal. Good fool, as ever thou wilt deserve well 90 at my hand, help me to a candle, and pen,

80. *"upshot"*; decision; a metaphor from archery, where the final shot which decided a match was so called.—C. H. H.

ink and paper: as I am a gentleman, I will live to be thankful to thee for 't.

Clo. Master Malvolio!

Mal. Aye, good fool.

Clo. Alas, sir, how fell you besides your five wits?

Mal. Fool, there was never man so notoriously abused: I am as well in my wits, fool, as thou art. 100

Clo. But as well? then you are mad indeed, if you be no better in your wits than a fool.

Mal. They have here propertied me; keep me in darkness, send ministers to me, asses, and do all they can to face me out of my wits.

Clo. Advise you what you say; the minister is here. Malvolio, Malvolio, thy wits the heavens restore! endeavor thyself to sleep, and leave thy vain bibble babble.

Mal. Sir Topas,— 110

Clo. Maintain no words with him, good fellow. Who, I, sir? not I, sir. God be wi' you, good Sir Topas. Marry, amen. I will, sir, I will.

Mal. Fool, fool, fool, I say,—

Clo. Alas, sir, be patient. What say you, sir? I am shent for speaking to you.

Mal. Good fool, help me to some light and some

105. *"face"*; bully.—C. H. H.

106. *"the minister is here"*; the Clown, in the dark, acts two persons, and counterfeits, by variation of voice, a dialogue between himself and Sir Topas; the preceding part of this speech being spoken as Clown, the following as Priest.—H. N. H.

paper: I tell thee, I am as well in my wits as
any man in Illyria. 120

Clo. Well-a-day that you were, sir!

Mal. By this hand, I am. Good fool, some
ink, paper and light; and convey what I
will set down to my lady: it shall advantage
thee more than ever the bearing of letter did.

Clo. I will help you to 't. But tell me true, are
you not mad indeed? or do you but counterfeit?

Mal. Believe me, I am not; I tell thee true.

Clo. Nay, I 'll ne'er believe a madman till I see 130
his brains. ~~I will fetch you light and paper
and ink.~~

Mal. Fool, I 'll requite it in the highest degree:
I prithee, be gone.

Clo. [*Singing*] I am gone, sir.
And anon, sir,
I 'll be with you again,
In a trice,
Like to the old vice,
Your need to sustain;
Who, with dagger of lath,
In his rage and his wrath,
Cries, ah, ha! to the devil:
Like a mad lad,
Pare thy nails, dad;
Adieu, goodman devil.

146. *"goodman devil"*; Folio 1, *"good man diuell"*; Rowe's *"goodman Drivel,"* seems the most plausible emendation, if any is necessary; Folio 2 reads *"good man Direll."*—I. G.

SCENE III

Olivia's garden.

Enter Sebastian.

Seb. This is the air; that is the glorious sun;
This pearl she gave me, I do feel 't and see 't;
And though 'tis wonder that enwraps me thus,
Yet 'tis not madness. Where 's Antonio, then?
I could not find him at the Elephant:
Yet there he was; and there I found this credit,
That he did range the town to seek me out.
His counsel now might do me golden service;
For though my soul disputes well with my sense,
That this may be some error, but no madness, 10
Yet doth this accident and flood of fortune
So far exceed all instance, all discourse,
That I am ready to distrust mine eyes
And wrangle with my reason, that persuades me
To any other trust but that I am mad,
Or else the lady's mad; yet, if 'twere so,
She could not sway her house, command her followers,
Take and give back affairs and their dispatch
With such a smooth, discreet, and stable bearing 19
As I perceive she does: there 's something in 't
That is deceivable. But here the lady comes.

12. *"instance"*; example.—C. H. H.

Enter Olivia and Priest.

Oli. Blame not this haste of mine. If you mean
well,

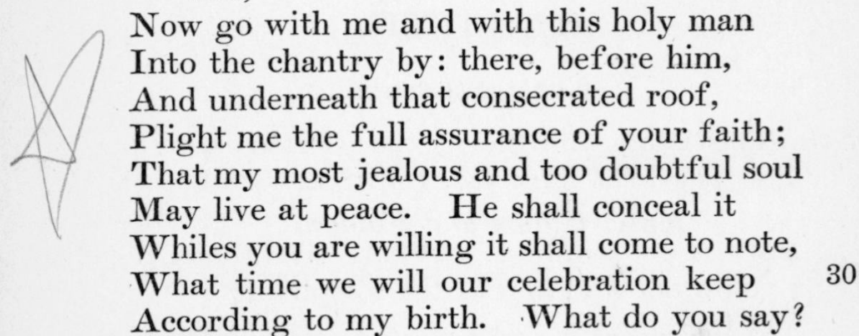

Now go with me and with this holy man
Into the chantry by: there, before him,
And underneath that consecrated roof,
Plight me the full assurance of your faith;
That my most jealous and too doubtful soul
May live at peace. He shall conceal it
Whiles you are willing it shall come to note,
What time we will our celebration keep 30
According to my birth. What do you say?

Seb. I 'll follow this good man, and go with you;
And having sworn truth, ever will be true.

Oli. Then lead the way, good father; and heavens
so shine,
That they may fairly note this act of mine!
[*Exeunt.*

33. *"sworn truth"; troth* or *fidelity.* It should be remarked that this was not an actual *marriage,* but a *betrothing,* affiancing, or solemn promise of future marriage; anciently distinguished by the name of *espousals.*—H. N. H.

ACT FIFTH

Scene I

Before Olivia's house.

Enter Clown and Fabian.

Fab. Now, as thou lovest me, let me see his letter.

Clo. Good Master Fabian, grant me another request.

Fab. Any thing.

Clo. Do not desire to see this letter.

Fab. This is, to give a dog, and in recompense desire my dog again.

Enter Duke, Viola, Curio, and Lords.

Duke. Belong you to the Lady Olivia, friends?

Clo. Aye, sir; we are some of her trappings. 10

Duke. I know thee well: how dost thou, my good fellow?

Clo. Truly, sir, the better for my foes and the worse for my friends.

Duke. Just the contrary; the better for thy friends.

Clo. No, sir, the worse.

Duke. How can that be?

10. *"trappings"*; appendages.—C. H. H.

Clo. Marry, sir, they praise me and make an ass of me; now my foes tell me plainly I am an ass: so that by my foes, sir, I profit in the knowledge of myself; and by my friends I am abused: so that, conclusions to be as kisses, if your four negatives make your two affirmatives, why then, the worse for my friends, and the better for my foes. 20

Duke. Why, this is excellent.

Clo. By my troth, sir, no; though it please you to be one of my friends.

Duke. Thou shalt not be the worse for me: there 's gold. 30

Clo. But that it would be double-dealing, sir, I would you could make it another.

Duke. O, you give me ill counsel.

Clo. Put your grace in your pocket, sir, for this once, and let your flesh and blood obey it.

Duke. Well, I will be so much a sinner, to be a double-dealer: there 's another.

Clo. Primo, secundo, tertio, is a good play; and the old saying is, the third pays for all: the triplex, sir, is a good tripping measure; or the bells of Saint Bennet, sir, may put you in mind; one, two, three. 40

Duke. You can fool no more money out of me at this throw: if you will let your lady know I am here to speak with her, and bring her along with you, it may awake my bounty further.

23. *"to be as"*; being as.—C. H. H.

Clo. Marry, sir, lullaby to your bounty till I 50
come again. I go, sir; but I would not
have you to think that my desire of having
is the sin of covetousness: but, as you say,
sir, let your bounty take a nap, I will awake
it anon. [*Exit.*

Vio. Here comes the man, sir, that did rescue
me.

Enter Antonio and Officers.

Duke. That face of his I do remember well;
Yet, when I saw it last, it was besmear'd
As black as Vulcan in the smoke of war: 60
A bawbling vessel was he captain of,
For shallow draught and bulk unprizable;
With which such scathful grapple did he make
With the most noble bottom of our fleet,
That very envy and the tongue of loss
Cried fame and honor on him. What 's the
matter?

First Off. Orsino, this is that Antonio
That took the Phœnix and her fraught from
Candy;
And this is he that did the Tiger board,
When your young nephew Titus lost his leg: 70
Here in the streets, desperate of shame and
state,
In private brabble did we apprehend him.

Vio. He did me kindness, sir, drew on my side;

63. *"scathful"*; harmful.—C. H. H.

65. *"the tongue of loss"*; the tongues of those on whom he had inflicted loss.—C. H. H.

But in conclusion put strange speech upon me:
I know not what 'twas but distraction.

Duke. Notable pirate! thou salt-water thief!
What foolish boldness brought thee to their mercies,
Whom thou, in terms so bloody and so dear,
Hast made thine enemies?

Ant. Orsino, noble sir,
Be pleased that I shake off these names you give me: 80
Antonio never yet was thief or pirate,
Though I confess, on base and ground enough,
Orsino's enemy. A witchcraft drew me hither:
That most ingrateful boy there by your side,
From the rude sea's enraged and foamy mouth
Did I redeem; a wreck past hope he was:
His life I gave him and did thereto add
My love, without retention or restraint,
All his in dedication; for his sake
Did I expose myself, pure for his love, 90
Into the danger of this adverse town;
Drew to defend him when he was beset:
Where being apprehended, his false cunning,
Not meaning to partake with me in danger,
Taught him to face me out of his acquaintance,
And grew a twenty years removed thing
While one would wink; denied me mine own purse,
Which I had recommended to his use
Not half an hour before.

95. *"face me"*; outface me.—C. H. H.

Vio. How can this be?
Duke. When came he to this town? 100
Ant. To-day, my lord; and for three months before,
No interim, not a minute's vacancy,
Both day and night did we keep company.

Enter Olivia and Attendants.

Duke. Here comes the countess: now heaven walks on earth.
But for thee, fellow; fellow, thy words are madness:
Three months this youth hath tended upon me;
But more of that anon. Take him aside.
Oli. What would my lord, but that he may not have,
Wherein Olivia may seem serviceable?
Cesario, you do not keep promise with me. 110
Vio. Madam!
Duke. Gracious Olivia,—
Oli. What do you say, Cesario? Good my lord,—
Vio. My lord would speak; my duty hushes me.
Oli. If it be aught to the old tune, my lord,
It is as fat and fulsome to mine ear
As howling after music.
Duke. Still so cruel?
Oli. Still so constant, lord.
Duke. What, to perverseness? you uncivil lady,
To whose ingrate and unauspicious altars 120
My soul the faithfull'st offerings hath breathed out

116. *"fat"*; heavy, dull.—C. H. H.
121. *"My soul the faithfull'st offerings hath breathed out"*; the

That e'er devotion tender'd! What shall I do?

Oli. Even what it please my lord, that shall become him.

Duke. Why should I not, had I the heart to do it,
Like to the Egyptian thief at point of death,
Kill what I love?—a savage jealousy
That sometime savors nobly. But hear me this:
Since you to non-regardance cast my faith,
And that I partly know the instrument
That screws me from my true place in your favor, 130
Live you the marble-breasted tyrant still;
But this your minion, whom I know you love,
And whom, by heaven I swear, I tender dearly,
Him will I tear out of that cruel eye,
Where he sits crowned in his master's spite.
Come, boy, with me; my thoughts are ripe in mischief:
I'll sacrifice the lamb that I do love,
To spite a raven's heart within a dove.

Folios *"haue,"* corrected by Capell, but probably Shakespeare's own reading; the plural for the singular, owing to the plural object (*"faithfull'st offerings"*) preceding the verb.—I. G.

126. *"Kill what I love"*; an allusion to the story of *"Thyamis,* as told by Heliodorus in his *Ethiopics,* of which an English version by Thomas Underdowne was published a second time in 1587. Thyamis was a native of Memphis, and chief of a band of robbers. Chariclea, a Greek, having fallen into his hands, he grew passionately in love with her, and would have married her: but being surprised by a stronger band of robbers, and knowing he must die, he went to the cave where he had secreted her with his other treasures, and, seizing her by the hair with his left hand, with his right plunged a sword in her breast; it being the custom with those barbarians, when they despaired of their own life, first to kill those whom they held most dear, so as to have them as companions in the other world.—H. N. H.

Vio. And I, most jocund, apt and willingly,
To do you rest, a thousand deaths would die.
Oli. Where goes Cesario?
Vio. After him I love 141
More than I love these eyes, more than my life,
More, by all mores, than e'er I shall love wife.
If I do feign, you witnesses above
Punish my life for tainting of my love!
Oli. Aye me, detested! how am I beguiled!
Vio. Who does beguile you? who does do you wrong?
Oli. Hast thou forgot thyself? is it so long?
Call forth the holy father.
Duke. Come, away!
Oli. Whither, my lord? Cesario, husband, stay.
Duke. Husband!
Oli. Aye, husband: can he that deny? 151
Duke. Her husband, sirrah!
Vio. No, my lord, not I.
Oli. Alas, it is the baseness of thy fear
That makes thee strangle thy propriety:
Fear not, Cesario; take thy fortunes up;
Be that thou know'st thou art, and then thou art
As great as that thou fear'st.

Enter Priest.

O, welcome, father!
Father, I charge thee, by thy reverence,
Here to unfold, though lately we intended

139. *"jocund, apt and willingly"*; the adverbial suffix of the last adjective does duty with all three.—C. H. H.
140. *"To do you rest"*; to give you rest of mind.—C. H. H.

To keep in darkness what occasion now 160
Reveals before 'tis ripe, what thou dost know
Hath newly pass'd between this youth and me.

Priest. A contract of eternal bond of love,
Confirm'd by mutual joinder of your hands,
Attested by the holy close of lips,
Strengthen'd by interchangement of your rings;
And all the ceremony of this compact
Seal'd in my function, by my testimony:
Since when, my watch hath told me, toward my grave
I have travel'd but two hours. 170

Duke. O thou dissembling cub! what wilt thou be
When time hath sow'd a grizzle on thy case?
Or will not else thy craft so quickly grow,
That thine own trip shall be thine overthrow?
Farewell, and take her; but direct thy feet
Where thou and I henceforth may never meet.

Vio. My lord, I do protest—

Oli. O, do not swear!
Hold little faith, though thou hast too much fear.

Enter Sir Andrew.

Sir And. For the love of God, a surgeon!
Send one presently to Sir Toby. 180

Oli. What 's the matter?

Sir And. He has broke my head across and has given Sir Toby a bloody coxcomb too: for the love of God, your help! I had rather than forty pound I were at home.

Oli. Who has done this, Sir Andrew?

Sir And. The count's gentleman, one Cesario: we took him for a coward, but he 's the very devil incardinate.

Duke. My gentleman, Cesario? 190

Sir And. 'Od's lifelings, here he is! You broke my head for nothing; and that that I did, I was set on to do 't by Sir Toby.

Vio. Why do you speak to me? I never hurt you:
You drew your sword upon me without cause;
But I bespake you fair, and hurt you not.

Sir And. If a bloody coxcomb be a hurt, you have hurt me: I think you set nothing by a bloody coxcomb.

Enter Sir Toby and Clown.

Here comes Sir Toby halting; you shall 200 hear more: but if he had not been in drink, he would have tickled you other gates than he did.

Duke. How now, gentleman! how is 't with you?

Sir To. That 's all one: has hurt me, and there 's the end on 't. Sot, didst see Dick surgeon, sot?

Clo. O, he 's drunk, Sir Toby, an hour agone; his eyes were set at eight i' the morning. 210

Sir To. Then he 's a rogue, and a passy measures pavin: I hate a drunken rogue.

189. *"incardinate"*; incarnate.—C. H. H.

198. *"set nothing by"*; take no account of.—C. H. H.

211. *"a passy measures pavin"*; Folio 1, *"panyn"*; Folio 2, *"Pavin"*; various emendations have been suggested, but there is

Oli. Away with him! Who hath made this havoc with them?

Sir And. I 'll help you, Sir Toby, because we 'll be dressed together.

Sir To. Will you help? an ass-head and a coxcomb and a knave, a thin-faced knave, a gull!

Oli. Get him to bed, and let his hurt be look'd to. [*Exeunt Clown, Fabian, Sir Toby and Sir Andrew.* 220

Enter Sebastian.

Seb. I am sorry, madam, I have hurt your kinsman;
But, had it been the brother of my blood,
I must have done no less with wit and safety.
You throw a strange regard upon me, and by that
I do perceive it hath offended you:
Pardon me, sweet one, even for the vows
We made each other but so late ago.

Duke. One face, one voice, one habit, and two persons,
A natural perspective, that is and is not! 230

Seb. Antonio, O my dear Antonio!

little doubt that the reading in the text is the correct one. *"Passy measures"* is a corruption of the Italian *"passamezzo,"* which word Florio explains as "a *passa-measure* in dancing, a cinque pace"; it was a slow dance, differing little from the action of walking. *"Pavin"* was a grave Spanish dance. According to Halliwell, the *passy measures pavin* is described as follows in an early MS. list of dances:—*"The passinge measure Pavyon*—2 singles and a double forward, and 2 singles syde.—Reprince back." Sir Toby means, therefore, that "the surgeon is a rogue and a grave solemn coxcomb." —I. G.

How have the hours rack'd and tortured me,
Since I have lost thee!

Ant. Sebastian are you?

Seb. Fear'st thou that, Antonio?

Ant. How have you made division of yourself?
An apple, cleft in two, is not more twin
Than these two creatures. Which is Sebastian?

Oli. Most wonderful!

Seb. Do I stand there? I never had a brother;
Nor can there be that deity in my nature, 240
Of here and every where. I had a sister,
Whom the blind waves and surges have devour'd.
Of charity, what kin are you to me?
What countryman? what name? what parentage?

Vio. Of Messaline: Sebastian was my father;
Such a Sebastian was my brother too,
So went he suited to his watery tomb:
If spirits can assume both form and suit,
You come to fright us.

Seb. A spirit I am indeed;
But am in that dimension grossly clad 250
Which from the womb I did participate.
Were you a woman, as the rest goes even,
I should my tears let fall upon your cheek,
And say 'Thrice-welcome, drowned Viola!'

Vio. My father had a mole upon his brow.

Seb. And so had mine.

Vio. And died that day when Viola from her birth

234. "*fear'st*"; doubtest.—C. H. H.
250. "*grossly*"; substantially.—C. H. H.

Had number'd thirteen years.
Seb. O, that record is lively in my soul!
He finished indeed his mortal act 260
That day that made my sister thirteen years.
Vio. If nothing lets to make us happy both
But this my masculine usurp'd attire,
Do not embrace me till each circumstance
Of place, time, fortune, do cohere and jump
That I am Viola: which to confirm,
I 'll bring you to a captain in this town,
Where lie my maiden weeds; by whose gentle help
I was preserved to serve this noble count.
All the occurrence of my fortune since 270
Hath been between this lady and this lord.
Seb. [*To Olivia*] So comes it, lady, you have been mistook:
But nature to her bias drew in that. character
You would have been contracted to a maid;
Nor are you therein, by my life, deceived,
You are betroth'd both to a maid and man.
Duke. Be not amazed; right noble is his blood.
If this be so, as yet the glass seems true,
I shall have share in this most happy wreck.
[*To Viola*] Boy, thou hast said to me a thousand times 280
Thou never shouldst love woman like to me.
Vio. And all those sayings will I over-swear;
And all those swearings keep as true in soul
As doth that orbed continent the fire
That severs day from night.
Duke. Give me thy hand;

And let me see thee in thy woman's weeds.

Vio. The captain that did bring me first on shore
Hath my maid's garments: he upon some action
Is now in durance, at Malvolio's suit,
A gentleman, and follower of my lady's. 290

Oli. He shall enlarge him: fetch Malvolio hither:
And yet, alas, now I remember me,
They say, poor gentleman, he 's much distract.

Re-enter Clown with a letter, and Fabian.

A most extracting frenzy of mine own
From my remembrance clearly banish'd his.
How does he, sirrah?

Clo. Truly, madam, he holds Belzebub at the stave's end as well as a man in his case may do: has here writ a letter to you; I should have given 't you to-day morning, but as a 300 madman's epistles are no gospels, so it skills not much when they are delivered.

Oli. Open 't and read it.

Clo. Look then to be well edified when the fool delivers the madman. [*Reads*] By the Lord, madam,—

Oli. How now! art thou mad?

Clo. No, madam, I do but read madness: an your ladyship will have it as it ought to be, you must allow Vox. 310

Oli. Prithee, read i' thy right wits.

Clo. So I do, madonna; but to read his right

305. *"delivers"*; reads the message of.—C. H. H.
310. *"Vox"*; the proper tone of voice.—C. H. H.

wits is to read thus: therefore perpend, my princess, and give ear.

Oli. Read it you, sirrah. [*To Fabian.*

Fab. By the Lord, madam, you wrong me and the world shall know it: though you have put me into darkness and given your drunken cousin rule over me, yet have I the benefit of my senses as well as your ladyship. I have your own letter that induced me to the semblance I put on; with the which I doubt n t but to do myself much right, or you much shame. Think of me as you please. I leave my duty a little unthought of, and speak out of my injury. 320

THE MADLY-USED MALVOLIO.

Oli. Did he write this?

Clo. Aye, madam.

Duke. This savors not much of distraction. 330

Oli. See him deliver'd, Fabian; bring him hither.

[*Exit Fabian.*

My lord, so please you, these things further thought on,
To think me as well a sister as a wife,
One day shall crown the alliance on 't, so please you,
Here at my house and at my proper cost.

Duke. Madam, I am most apt to embrace your offer.
[*To Viola*] Your master quits you; and for your service done him,
So much against the mettle of your sex,

337. *"quits you"*; sets you free.—C. H. H.

So far beneath your soft and tender breeding,
And since you call'd me master for so long, 340
Here is my hand: you shall from this time be
Your master's mistress.

Oli. A sister! you are she.

Re-enter Fabian, with Malvolio.

Duke. Is this the madman?

Oli. Aye, my lord, this same.
How now, Malvolio!

Mal. Madam, you have done me wrong,
Notorious wrong.

Oli. Have I, Malvolio? no.

Mal. Lady, you have. Pray you, peruse that letter.
You must not now deny it is your hand:
Write from it, if you can, in hand or phrase;
Or say 'tis not your seal, not your invention:
You can say none of this: well, grant it then
And tell me, in the modesty of honor, 351
Why you have given me such clear lights of favor,
Bade me come smiling and cross-garter'd to you,
To put on yellow stockings and to frown
Upon Sir Toby and the lighter people;
And, acting this in an obedient hope,
Why have you suffer'd me to be imprison'd,
Kept in a dark house, visited by the priest,
And made the most notorious geck and gull
That e'er invention play'd on? tell me why. 360

348. *"Write from it"*; write unlike it.—C. H. H.

Oli. Alas, Malvolio, this is not my writing,
Though, I confess, much like the character:
But out of question 'tis Maria's hand.
And now I do bethink me, it was she
First told me thou wast mad; then camest in smiling,
And in such forms which here were presupposed
Upon thee in the letter. Prithee, be content:
This practice hath most shrewdly pass'd upon thee;
But when we know the grounds and authors of it,
Thou shalt be both the plaintiff and the judge
Of thine own cause.

Fab. Good madam, hear me speak,
And let no quarrel nor no brawl to come 372
Taint the condition of this present hour,
Which I have wonder'd at. In hope it shall not,
Most freely I confess, myself and Toby
Set this device against Malvolio here,
Upon some stubborn and uncourteous parts
We had conceived against him: Maria writ
The letter at Sir Toby's great importance;
In recompense whereof he hath married her.
How with a sportful malice it was follow'd 381
May rather pluck on laughter than revenge;
If that the injuries be justly weigh'd
That have on both sides pass'd.

Oli. Alas, poor fool, how have they baffled thee!

378. *"against"*; Tyrwhitt's conjecture *"in"* has a good deal in its favor; *"against"* may have been caught from the line 376.—I. G.

Clo. Why, 'some are born great, some achieve greatness, and some have greatness thrown upon them.' I was one, sir, in this interlude; one Sir Topas, sir; but that 's all one. 'By the Lord, fool, I am not mad.' But do 390 you remember? Madam, why laugh you at such a barren rascal? an you smile not, he 's gagged:' and thus the whirligig of time brings in his revenges.

Mal. I 'll be revenged on the whole pack of you. [*Exit.*

Oli. He hath been most notoriously abused.

Duke. Pursue him, and entreat him to a peace:
He hath not told us of the captain yet:
When that is known, and golden time convents,
A solemn combination shall be made 401
Of our dear souls. Meantime, sweet sister,
We will not part from hence. Cesario, come;
For so you shall be, while you are a man;
But when in other habits you are seen,
Orsino's mistress and his fancy's queen.

[*Exeunt all, except Clown*

Clo. [*Sings*]
When that I was and a little tiny boy,
With hey, ho, the wind and the rain,
A foolish thing was but a toy,
For the rain it raineth every day. 410

But when I came to man's estate,
With hey, ho, &c.
'Gainst knaves and thieves men shut their gate,
For the rain, &c.

409. *"toy"*; trifle.—C. H. H.

But when I came, alas! to wive,
  With hey, ho, &c.
By swaggering could I never thrive,
  For the rain, &c.

But when I came unto my beds,
  With hey, ho, &c. 420
With toss-pots still had drunken heads,
  For the rain, &c.

A great while ago the world begun,
  With hey, ho, &c.
But that 's all one, our play is done,
  And we 'll strive to please you every day.
[*Exit*.

421. *"toss-pots"*; drunkards.—C. H. H.

GLOSSARY

By Israel Gollancz, M.A.

Abuse, deceive; III. i. 127.

Accosted, addressed; III. ii. 24.

A degree, one step; III. i. 137.

Adheres, accords; III. iv. 89.

Admire, wonder; III. iv. 169.

Adverse, hostile; V. i. 91.

Advise you, take care; IV. ii. 106.

Affectioned, affected; II. iii. 168.

Agone, ago; V. i. 209.

Allowed, licensed; I. v. 107.

Allow me, make me acknowledged; I. ii. 59.

Alone, pre-eminently; I. i. 15.

An = one; II. i. 22.

Anatomy, body, used contemptuously; III. ii. 72.

And, used redundantly, as in the old ballads; V. i. 407.

Antique, quaint; II. iv. 3.

Apt, ready; V. i. 336.

Arbitrement, decision; III. iv. 294.

Argument, proof; III. ii. 13.

As yet, still; V. i. 278.

Attends, awaits; III. iv. 249.

Back-trick, a caper backwards; I. iii. 138.

Baffled, treated with contempt; V. i. 385.

Barful, full of impediments; (Pope, "O baneful"; Daniel, "a woeful"); I. iv. 42.

Barren, dull; I. v. 94.

Barricadoes, fortifications made in haste, obstructions; IV. ii. 43.

Bawbling, insignificant, trifling; V. i. 61.

Bawcock, a term of endearment; always used in masculine sense; III. iv. 130.

Beagle, a small dog; II. iii. 204.

Before me, by my soul; II. iii. 203.

Belike, I suppose; III. iii. 29.

Bent, tension; II. iv. 38.

Beshrew, a mild form of imprecation; IV. i. 63.

Besides, out of; IV. ii. 96.

Bespake you fair, spoke kindly to you; V. i. 196.

Bias, originally the weighted side of a bowl; V. i. 273.

Bibble babble, idle talk; IV. ii. 109.

Biddy, "a call to allure chickens"; III. iv. 133.

Bird-bolts, blunt-headed arrows; I. v. 105.

Blazon, "coat-of-arms"; I. v. 323.

Blent = blended; I. v. 268.

Bloody, bloodthirsty; III. iv. 248.

Blows, inflates, puffs up; II. v. 48.

Bosom, the folds of the dress covering the breast, stomacher; III. i. 135.

Botcher, mender of old clothes; I. v. 53.

Bottle-ale, bottled ale; II. iii. 31.

Bottom, ship, vessel; V. i. 64.

Brabble, brawl, broil; V. i. 72.

Branched, "adorned with needlework, representing flowers and twigs"; II. v. 54.

Breach, surf; II. i. 25.

Breast, voice; II. iii. 21.

Bred, begotten; I. ii. 22.

Brock, badger, a term of contempt; II. v. 116.

Brownist, a member of a Puritan sect; III. ii. 37.

Bum-baily, bailiff; III. iv. 198.

But = than; I. iv. 14.

Buttery-bar; buttery, place where drink and food were kept; *bar,* place where they were served out; I. iii. 78.

By the duello, by the laws of duelling; III. iv. 348.

Canary, wine from the Canary Isles; I. iii. 90.

Cantons = cantos; I. v. 300.

Case, body, skin; V. i. 172.

Castiliano vulgo, "Spanish of Sir Toby's own making," perhaps it may mean, "Be as reticent as a Castilian now that one of the common herd is coming"; I. iii. 48.

Cataian, Chinese; used here as a term of reproach; II. iii. 84.

Catch, "a song sung in succession"; II. iii. 19.

Chain; the chain of office which stewards were accustomed to wear; II. iii. 136.

Chantry, a private chapel; IV. iii. 24.

Checks; "to check" is "a term in falconry, applied to a hawk when she forsakes her proper game, and follows some other of inferior kind that crosses her in her flight"; II. v. 126; III. i. 72.

Cherry-pit, "a game consisting in pitching cherry-stones into a small hole"; III. iv. 134.

Cheveril, roe-buck leather; symbol of flexibility; III. i. 13.

Chuck, chicken, a term of endearment; III. iv. 131.

Civil, polite, well-mannered; III. iv. 5.

Clodpole, blockhead; III. iv. 213.

Cloistress, inhabitant of a cloister, nun; I. i. 28.

Cloyment, surfeit; II. iv. 103.

Cockatrice, an imaginary creature, supposed to be produced from a cock's egg, and to have so deadly an eye as to kill by its very look; III. iv. 220.

Collier; "the devil was called so because of his blackness"; *cp.* the proverb: *"like will to like, quoth the devil to the collier"*; III. iv. 135.

Colors; "fear no colors," fear no enemy; I. v. 11.

Comfortable, comforting; I. v. 2.

Commerce, conversation; III. iv. 195.

Compare, comparison; II. iv. 105.

Competitors, confederates; IV. ii. 12.

Complexion, external appearance; II. iv. 27.

Comptible, sensitive; I. v. 97.

Conceited, has formed an idea; III. iv. 332.

Conclusions to be as kisses, *i. e.* "as in a syllogism it takes two premises to make one conclusion, so it takes two people to make one kiss" (Cambridge edition); V. i. 23.

CONDUCT, guard, escort; III. iv. 271.

CONSEQUENTLY, subsequently; III. iv. 81.

CONSIDERATION; "on carpet c."= "a mere carpet knight"; III. iv. 263.

CONSTANT, consistent, logical; IV. ii. 56.

CONVENTS, is convenient; V. i. 400.

CORANTO, a quick, lively dance; I. iii. 147.

COUPLET, couple; III. iv. 421.

COXCOMB, head; V. i. 183.

COYSTRILL, a mean, paltry fellow; I. iii. 46.

COZIERS, botchers, cobblers; II. iii. 102.

CREDIT, intelligence; IV. iii. 6.

CROSS-GARTERED, alluding to the custom of wearing the garters crossed in various styles; II. v. 173.

CROWNER, coroner; I. v. 149.

CRUELTY, cruel one; II. iv. 84.

CUBICULO (one of Sir Toby's "affectioned" words), apartment; III. ii. 60.

"CUCULLUS NON FACIT MONACHUM"= a cowl does not make a monk; I. v. 64.

CUNNING, skillful; I. v. 269.

CURST, sharp, shrewish; III. ii. 48.

CUT, a docked horse; II. iii. 212.

CYPRESS, probably "a coffin of cypresswood"; (others explain it as a shroud of *cypress;* Cotgrave mentions *white cipres*); II. iv. 53.

CYPRESS, crape (*v.* Note); III. i. 135.

DALLY, play, trifle; III. i. 16.

DAY-BED, couch, sofa; II. v. 55.

DEADLY, death-like; I. v. 295.

DEAR, heartfelt; V. i. 78.

DECEIVABLE, delusive; IV. iii. 21.

DEDICATION, devotedness; V. i. 89.

DELIVER'D, set at liberty; V. i. 331.

DENAY, denial; II. iv. 128.

DENY, refuse; IV. i. 63.

DESPERATE, hopeless; II. ii. 8; reckless; V. i. 71.

DESPITE, malice; III. iv. 248.

DETERMINATE, fixed; II. i. 11.

DEXTERIOUSLY, dexterously; I. v. 69.

DILUCULO SURGERE (saluberrimum est), to rise early is most healthful; II. iii. 2.

DIMENSION, bodily shape; I. v. 291; V. i. 250.

DISCOURSE, reasoning; IV. iii. 12.

DISMOUNT, draw from the scabbard; III. iv. 249.

DISORDERS, misconduct; II. iii. 111.

DISSEMBLE, disguise; IV. ii. 5.

DISTEMPER, make ill-humored; II. i. 5.

DISTEMPERED, diseased; I. v. 103.

DRY, insipid; I. v. 46.

EGYPTIAN THIEF; an allusion to Thyamis, a robber chief in the Greek Romance of *Theagenes and Chariclea* (trans. into English before 1587); the thief attempted to kill Chariclea, whom he loved, rather than lose her; by mistake he slew another person; V. i. 125.

ELEMENT, sky and air; I. i. 26; sphere; III. i. 66.

ELEPHANT, the name of an inn; III. iii. 39.

Enchantment, love-charm; III. i. 126.

Encounter, go towards; used affectedly; III. i. 82.

Endeavor thyself, try; IV. ii. 108.

Enlarge, release; V. i. 291.

Entertainment, treatment; I. v. 241.

Estimable wonder, admiring judgment; II. i. 30.

Except, before excepted, alluding to the common law-phrase; I. iii. 7.

Expenses, a tip, douceur; III. i. 49.

Expressure, expression; II. iii. 180.

Extent, conduct, behavior; IV. i. 58.

Extracting (later Folios "exacting"), "drawing other thoughts from my mind"; V. i. 294.

Extravagancy, vagrancy; II. i. 12.

Fadge, prosper; II. ii. 35.

Fall, strain, cadence; I. i. 4.

Fancy, love; I. i. 14; V. i. 406.

Fantastical, fanciful, creative; I. i. 15.

"Farewell, dear heart, since I must needs begone," etc., altered from *Corydon's Farewell to Phillis* (Percy's *Reliques*); II. iii. 116.

Favor, face, form; II. iv. 24; III. iv. 374.

Feature, external form, body; III. iv. 410.

Feelingly, exactly; II. iii. 181.

Fellow, companion; III. iv. 87.

Firago, corruption of virago; III. iv. 310.

Fire-new, brand-new; III. ii. 25.

Fit, becoming, suitable; III. i. 75.

Flatter with, encourage with hopes; I. v. 333.

Fleshed, "made fierce and eager for combat, as a dog fed with flesh only"; IV. i. 44.

Fond, dote; II. ii. 36.

Forgive, excuse; I. v. 215.

For that, because; III. i. 168.

Fourteen years' purchase, *i. e.* "at a high rate," the current price in Shakespeare's time being twelve years' purchase; IV. i. 25.

Fraught, freight; V. i. 68.

Free, careless (or perhaps graceful, comely; *cp.* "fair and free"); II. iv. 46.

Fresh in murmur, begun to be rumored; I. ii. 32.

Fright, affright; V. i. 249.

From, "f. Candy," *i. e.* "on her voyage from Candy"; V. i. 68.

Fulsome, gross, distasteful; V. i. 112.

Galliard, a lively French dance; I. iii. 134.

Gaskins, a kind of loose breeches; I. v. 28.

Geck, dupe; V. i. 359.

Gentleness, kindness, good-will; II. i. 48.

Giddily, negligently; II. iv. 88.

Gin, snare; II. v. 93.

Ginger, a favorite spice in Shakespeare's time, especially with old people; frequently referred to by Shakespeare; II. iii. 133.

Goes even, agrees, tallies; V. i. 252.

Good Life, jollity, with a play upon the literal meaning of the word, "virtuous living"; II. iii. 42–44.

GOODMAN (Folios "good man"), a familiar appellation, sometimes used contemptuously; IV. ii. 146.

GRACE, virtue; V. i. 35.

GRACIOUS, full of graces; I. v. 292.

GRAIN, "in grain," natural; I. v. 266.

GRATILLITY, clown's blunder for "gratuity"; II. iii. 29.

GREEK; "foolish Greek," *i. e.* jester, merrymaker (*cp.* "Matthew Merrygreek" in *Ralph Roister Doister*); "the Greeks were proverbially spoken of by the Romans as fond of good living and free potations" (Nares); IV. i. 20.

GRIZE, step, degree; III. i. 138.

GRIZZLE, a tinge of gray (perhaps a grizzly beard); V. i. 172.

GUST = gusto, enjoyment; I. iii. 35.

HAGGARD, a wild untrained hawk; III. i. 72.

HALE, draw; III. ii. 68.

HAPLY, perhaps; IV. ii. 60.

HAVING, possessions; III. iv. 389.

HEAT, course; I. i. 26.

"HEY ROBIN, JOLLY ROBIN," etc., an old ballad (to be found in the *Reliques,* Percy); IV. ii. 82–83.

HIGH = highly; I. i. 15.

HOB NOB, "have or have not, hit or miss, at random"; III. iv. 268.

"HOLD THY PEACE, THOU KNAVE," an old three-part catch, so arranged that each singer calls the other "knave" in turn; II. iii. 72.

HONESTY, "decency, love of what is becoming"; II. iii. 99.

HORRIBLE, horribly; III. iv. 200.

HULL, float; I. v. 227.

HUMOR OF STATE, "capricious insolence of authority"; II. v. 59.

IDLENESS, frivolousness; I. v. 73.

IMPETICOS, to impocket, or impetticoat; one of the clown's nonsense words; II. iii. 29.

IMPORTANCE, importunity; V. i. 379.

IMPRESSURE, impression; II. v. 104.

INCENSEMENT, exasperation; III. iv. 265.

INCREDULOUS, incredible; III. iv. 91.

INGRATEFUL, ungrateful; V. i. 84.

INTERCHANGEMENT, interchange; V. i. 166.

INTO, unto; V. i. 91.

JEALOUSY, apprehension; III. iii. 8.

JETS, struts; II. v. 35.

JEWEL, a piece of jewelry; III. iv. 233.

JEZEBEL, used vaguely as a term of reproach; II. v. 46.

JOINDER, joining; V. i. 164.

JUMP, tally; V. i. 265.

KICKSHAWSES = kickshaws; I. iii. 129.

KINDNESS, tenderness; II. i. 43.

LAPSED, surprised; III. iii. 36.

LATE, lately; I. ii. 30; III. i. 42.

LEASING, lying; I. v. 110.

LEMAN, lover, sweetheart; II. iii. 28.

LENTEN, scanty, poor; I. v. 9.

LETS, hinders; V. i. 262.
LIES, dwells; III. i. 8.
LIGHTER, inferior in position; V. i. 355.
LIMED, caught with bird-lime, ensnared; III. iv. 84.
LIST, boundary, limit; III. i. 86.
LITTLE, a little; V. i. 178.
LIVER, popularly supposed to be the seat of the emotions; II. iv. 102; III. ii. 23.
LOVE-BROKER, agent between lovers; III. ii. 42.
LOWLY, mean, base; III. i. 113.
LULLABY, "good night"; V. i. 50.

MAIDENHEAD = maidenhood; I. v. 243.
MALAPERT, saucy, forward; IV. i. 48.
MALIGNANCY, malevolence; II. i. 4.
MAUGER, in spite of; III. i. 165.
MEDDLE, fight; III. iv. 282.
METAL (Folio 1, "mettle"; Folio 2, "nettle"); "metal of India" = "my golden girl, my jewel"; (others explain "nettle of India" as the *Urtica marina,* a plant of itching properties); II. v. 16.
MINION, favorite, darling; V. i. 132.
MINX, *a pert woman;* III. iv. 138.
MISCARRY, be lost, die; III. iv. 70.
MISPRISION, misapprehension; I. v. 63.
MISTRESS MALL; probably "a mere personification," like "my lady's eldest son" in *Much Ado;* I. iii. 142.
MOLLIFICATION; "some m. for your giant," *i. e.* "something to pacify your gigantic (!) waiting-maid"; I. v. 228.
MONSTER, unnatural creature; II. ii. 36.
MORTAL, deadly; III. iv. 294.
MOUSE, a term of endearment; I. v. 72.

NAYWORD, by-word; II. iii. 153.
NEWLY, lately; V. i. 162.
NICELY, sophistically, subtilely; III. i. 16.
NON-REGARDANCE, disregard; V. i. 128.
NOT, used pleonastically after "forbid"; II. ii. 20.
NOTE; "come to note," *i. e.* "become known"; IV. iii. 29.
NOTORIOUS, notable; V. i. 345.
NUMBERS, measure of the verses; II. v. 114.
NUNCIO, messenger; I. iv. 29.

OF = on; III. iv. 2; for the sake of; V. i. 243.
ON = at; II. ii. 3.
OPAL, a precious stone supposed to change its colors; II. iv. 77.
OPEN, openly; III. iii. 37.
OPPOSITE, opponent; III. ii. 73; III. iv. 258.
OPPOSITE, hostile; II. v. 167.
ORB, earth; III. i. 43.
ORBED CONTINENT, the sun; V. i. 284.
OTHER GATES, in another way; V. i. 202.
"O, THE TWELFTH DAY OF DECEMBER," the opening of some old ballad now lost; II. iii. 95.
OVER-SWEAR, repeat, swear over again; V. i. 282.
OWE = own; I. v. 340.

PARISH-TOP, alluding to the large top kept in every village, for the peasants to whip in frosty weather, for the purpose of keeping themselves warm and out of mischief; I. iii. 48.

PART, in part, partly; III. iv. 387.

PASSAGES, acts; III. ii. 82.

PASS UPON (literally, to thrust), to make a push in fencing; make sallies of wit; III. i. 48.

PEDANT, schoolmaster; III. ii. 85.

PEEVISH, silly, willful; I. v. 330.

"PEG-A-RAMSAY," the name of an old ballad now unknown; III. iii. 85.

PENTHESILEA, the queen of the Amazons; II. iii. 202.

PERCHANCE, by chance; I. ii. 6.

PERDY, a corruption of *Par Dieu;* IV. ii. 85.

PERPEND, attend, listen; V. i. 314.

PERSONAGE, personal appearance; I. v. 172.

PERSPECTIVE, deception; V. i. 230.

PILCHARD, a fish strongly resembling the herring; III. i. 39.

PIPE, voice; I. iv. 33.

"PLEASE ONE, AND PLEASE ALL"; the title of an old ballad (entered on the Stationers' Registers in Jan. 18, 1591-92; printed in Staunton's *Shakespeare*); III. iv. 25.

PLUCK ON, excite; V. i. 382.

POINT-DEVISE, exactly; II. v. 183.

POSSESS US, puts us in possession, tell us; II. iii. 157.

POST, messenger: I. v. 314.

PRACTISE, plot; V. i. 368.

PRAISE = appraise; (perhaps (?) with a play upon the two senses of *praise*); I. v. 279.

PRANKS, adorns; II. iv. 90.

PREGNANT, clever, expert; II. ii, 30; III. i. 101.

PRESENT, *i. e.* present wealth; III. iv. 390.

PRESENTLY, immediately; III. iv. 222.

PREVENTED, anticipated; III. i. 94.

PRIVATE, privacy; III. iv. 104.

PROBATION, examination; II. v. 145.

PROOF; "vulgar p." common experience; III. i. 138.

PROPER, handsome; III. i. 147; own; V. i. 335.

PROPER-FALSE, "well-looking and deceitful"; II. ii. 31.

PROPERTIED, taken possession of; IV. ii. 103.

PROPRIETY, individuality, thyself; V. i. 154.

PURE, purely; V. i. 90.

QUESTION; "in contempt of q." past question; II. v. 99.

QUICK, living; lively; I. i. 9.

QUINAPALUS, an imaginary philosopher; I. v. 40.

QUIRK, humor; caprice; III. iv. 275.

RECEIVING, understanding, quick wit; III. i. 134.

RECOLLECTED, variously interpreted to mean (1) studied; (2) refined; (3) trivial; "recollected terms" perhaps = popular refrains (?) "terms" = "turns" or "tunes"); II. iv. 5.

RECORD, memory; V. i. 259.

RECOVER, win; II. iii. 209.

REGARD, look, glance; V. i. 225.

REINS, is governed by the bridle; III. iv. 369.

RELIQUES, memorials; III. iii. 19.

RENOWN, make famous; III. iii. 24.

REVERBERATE, reverberating, echoing; I. v. 302.

ROUND, plain; II. iii. 108.

Rub with crums, to clean; II. iii. 135.

Rubious, red, rosy; I. iv. 33.

Rudesby, blusterer; IV. i. 56.

Rule, behavior; II. iii. 139.

Sack, Spanish and Canary wine; II. iii. 215.

Sad, serious; III. iv. 5.

Saint Bennet, probably St. Bennet's, Paul's Wharf, London, destroyed in the great fire; V i. 43.

Scab, a term of reproach or dis gust; II. v. 83.

Scout, watch; III. iv. 197.

Self, self-same (perhaps with the force of "exclusive," "absolute"); I. i. 39.

Semblative, seeming, like; I. iv 35.

"Shake your ears," an expres sion of contempt, "grumble your pleasure"; II. iii. 141.

She, woman; I. v. 270.

Sheep-biter, a cant term for thief; II. v. 6.

Shent, chidden; IV. ii. 117.

Sheriff's post; alluding to the custom of sheriffs setting up posts at their doors, upon which to place notices an(proclamations; I. v. 164.

Shrewishly, pertly; I. v. 178.

Silly sooth, simple truth; II. iv. 47.

Sir, gentleman, lord; III. iv. 84; title formerly applied to the inferior clergy; IV. ii. 2.

Skilless, inexperienced; III. iii. 9.

Skills, matters; V. i. 301.

Skipping, wild, mad; I. v. 225.

'Slid, a corruption of "by God's lid"; III. iv. 437.

'Slight, a corruption of "God's light"; II. v. 37; III. ii. 15.

Sneck up, an exclamation of contempt; go and be hanged; II. iii. 107.

Sophy, Shah of Persia; II. v. 206; III. iv. 316.

Sound, clear; I. iv. 34.

Sowter, name of a hound; II. v. 138.

Spinsters, female spinners; II. iv. 45.

Spoke, said; I. iv. 21.

Squash, an immature peascod; I. v. 174.

Stable, steady; IV. iii. 19.

Standing water, between the ebb and flood of the tide; I. v. 176.

Staniel (Folios, "stallion," corrected by Hanmer, a kind of hawk; II. v. 126.

State = condition, fortune; I. v. 308; V. i. 71.

State, chair of State; II. v. 50.

Stitches, a sharp pain; III. ii. 78.

Stock, stocking; I. iii. 152.

Stone-bow, "a cross-bow, from which stones or bullets were shot"; II. v. 51.

Stroup, a drinking vessel; II. iii. 136.

Strange, estranged; V. i. 225.

Strange, stout, reserved and proud; II. v. 193.

Strangeness, reserve; IV. i. 17.

Strangle, suppress; V. i. 154.

Stuck, stoccato, a thrust in fencing; III. iv. 312.

Substractors; Sir Toby's blunder for "detractors"; I. iii. 39.

Suited, clad; V. i. 247.

Supportance, upholding; III. iv. 339.

Swabber, one who scrubs the ship's deck; I. v. 227.

Swarths, swaths; II. iii. 170.
Sweeting, a term of endearment; II. iii. 46.

Tabor, an instrument used by professional clowns; III. i. 2.
Taffeta, a fine smooth stuff of silk; II. iv. 77.
Tainting of, bringing discredit upon; V. i. 145.
Take up, acknowledge; V. i. 155.
Tall, used ironically; I. iii. 22.
Tang, twang; II. v. 168.
Tartar, Tartarus; II. v. 235.
Taste, put to use, try; III. i. 87.
Taxation, tax, demand; I. v. 235.
Tender, hold dear; V. i. 133.
Terms, words, *vide* "recollected terms"; II. iv. 5.
Testril, sixpence; II. iii. 37.
"There dwelt a man in Babylon," a line from the old ballad of *Susanna*; II. ii. 88.
"Three merry men be we," a fragment of an old song; frequently quoted by the dramatists (*cp.* Chappell's *Popular Music*); II. iii. 85.
Throw, a throw with the dice, hence "cast, or venture"; V. i. 46.
Tillyvally, an exclamation of contempt; II. iii. 87.
Time-pleaser, time-server, flatterer; II. iii. 168.
Tinkers, menders of old brass; "proverbial tipplers and would-be politicians"; II. iii. 100.
Trade, business; III. i. 83.
Travel of regard, looking about; II. v. 60.
Tray-trip, a game like backgammon; II. v. 216.
Trouble; "your tr." the trouble I have caused you; II. i. 37.
Trunks, alluding to the elaborately carved chests in use in Shakespeare's time; III. iv. 414.
Tuck, rapier; III. iv. 250.

Unauspicious, inauspicious; V. i. 120.
Unchary, heedlessly; III. iv. 227.
Ungird, relax; IV. i. 17.
Unhatched, "unhacked, not blunted by blows"; III. iv. 262.
Unprizable, invaluable; V. i. 62.
Unprofited, profitless; I. iv. 23.
Upon, because of, in consequence of; V. i. 377.
Use, usury; III. i. 57.

Validity, value; I. i. 12.
Venerable, worthy of veneration; III. iv. 407.
Vice, the buffoon of the old morality plays; IV. ii. 139.
Viol-de-gamboys; Sir Toby's blunder for *viol da gamba,* a base-viol or violoncello, a fashionable instrument of that time; I. iii. 29.
Vouchsafed, vouchsafing; III. i. 101.

Wainropes, wagon-ropes; III. ii. 68.
Ware; "Bed of Ware"; a huge bed, capable of holding twelve persons; formerly at the Saracen's Head Inn at Ware, and now at the Rye-House; III. ii. 55.
Was, had been; IV. iii. 6.
Waters; "I am for all waters," *i. e.* "I can turn my hand to anything; like a fish, I can swim equally well in all waters"; IV. ii. 71.
Weaver, alluding perhaps to the

psalm-singing propensities of the weavers; II. iii. 65.

WEEDS, garments; V. i. 268.

WELKIN, sky; II. iii. 62; III. i. 65.

WELL-A-DAY, an exclamation expressive of grief; "welaway," alas! IV. ii. 121.

WERE BEST, had better; III. iv. 12.

WERE BETTER, had better; II. ii. 28.

"WESTWARD-HO!" an exclamation often used by the boatmen on the Thames; III. i. 148.

WHAT, at which; IV. iii. 30.

WHAT'S SHE = who is she; I. ii. 35.

WHILES = while; III. iii. 41; until; IV. iii. 29.

WHIPSTOCK, whip-handle; II. iii. 30.

WINDY, safe; III. iv. 185.

WITH, by; I. v. 95.

WITS; "five wits," *viz.* "common wit, imagination, fantasy, estimation, and memory"; IV. ii. 97.

WOODCOCK; a bird popularly supposed to have no brains, hence the word was commonly used for a fool; II. v. 93; IV. ii. 67.

WORTH, substance, wealth; III. iii. 17.

YARE, ready, active; III. iv. 250.

"YEOMAN OF THE WARDROBE," a regular title of office in Shakespeare's time; II. v. 44.

ZANIES, "subordinate buffoons whose office was to make awkward attempts at mimicking the tricks of the professional clown"; I. v. 101.

STUDY QUESTIONS

By Emma D. Sanford

GENERAL

1. What is the condition of the text, from a literary standpoint?

2. Give one authority for the date of composition.

3. What is the English title of the two Italian plays from which Shakespeare may have derived his plot? Mention another more probable source.

4. Give the usual interpretation of the title of the play. Mention other Shakespearean plays which contain the element of *disguise*.

ACT I

5. In the opening lines of the play, what key is given to that artistic feature on which this play depends, for its charm?

6. What is the quibble intended on "hunting" the "hart"?

7. Explain the simile, "like Arion on the dolphin's back" (scene ii).

8. Why did Viola take service under the Duke, although she appears to have some means of her own?

9. Note Viola's claim to musical accomplishments (see Question 5 for its application).

10. Comment on the conversational merits of Sir Toby, Maria and Aguecheek; how do they differ from that of such characters as Viola, Olivia and the Duke?

11. What new element is introduced to the play's action in scene iii?

12. What speech, by the Duke, indicates that he has no confidence in his own ability to woo Olivia (scene iv)?

13. In the closing lines of scene iv, what does Viola confess?

14. In scene v, give a reason for the importance of the Clown, as a character of the play.

15. What idea does Olivia furnish as to Malvolio's disposition?

16. How does scene v give Viola an opportunity to give vent to her natural disposition?

17. Why does Olivia give Viola a chance to return? Has the Duke's messenger furthered, or injured his suit, and why?

18. Recall another play where Shakespeare makes a woman fall in love with another woman disguised as a man. What is the dramatic inference?

ACT II

19. Does scene i furnish us with any new addition to the plot?

20. What trick does Olivia play upon Viola (scene ii)?

21. Are the songs, snatches of which are sung by the Clown and Sir Toby, inventions or songs of the period?

22. Explain "three souls out of one weaver" (scene iii).

23. What joke does Maria plan to play on Malvolio? Why does she dislike him?

24. In scene iv, is Viola purposely endeavoring to discourage the Duke in his suit to Olivia?

25. Explain the reference by Malvolio to "yellow stockings" (scene V).

26. In the letter read aloud by Malvolio, select an epigram which has been very commonly quoted in literature.

27. What mental quality is absolutely lacking in Malvolio?

ACT III

28. How do Viola's comments on the wisdom of a fool seem particularly appropriate to this play?

29. How does the episode of the ring furnish the theme for the second interview between Olivia and Viola?

30. After having refused the Duke's suit, why does Olivia hold forth a hope to Viola that he may yet win her?

31. What reason does Sir Andrew give for his despair at winning Olivia for a wife; how does this furnish an occasion for a future comic episode?

32. Explain "if thou thou'st him" (scene ii).

33. Is there any trace of satire in placing Malvolio in such a ridiculous situation?

34. What interesting situations arouse the reader to great expectations, at the close of scene ii?

35. Why is the plot complicated by the arrival of Sebastian?

36. How do Maria and the two knights continue to make sport of Malvolio?

37. What challenge does Sir Andrew make Viola (scene iv)?

38. How does Sir Toby hope to prevent a genuine duel?

39. Has Olivia given much proof of a sincere grief for the loss of her brother? Why?

40. Why does Sir Andrew gather courage to fight Viola, after trying to buy her off?

41. What does the resemblance of Viola to her brother prepare us for (scene iv)?

ACT IV

42. Note Sebastian's generosity to the Clown, and that of his sister toward the Captain; what does this argue?

43. Who interrupts the encounter between Sir Toby and Sebastian?

44. Why does Olivia invite Sebastian to her house?

45. Explain the Clown's jest at Malvolio and the soul of his grandmother.

46. In scene ii, what double rôle does the Clown assume?

47. Why does Sir Toby lose interest in the sport at Malvolio?

48. Give a reason for Sebastian's pleasure in his marriage to Olivia, in spite of the fact that he feels confident that there is something unnatural in the situation.

ACT V

49. Why is the character of Antonio a necessary one in the last Act?

50. Does Orsino know of Olivia's marriage when he accuses Viola of having played him false?

51. What dramatic episode serves as an entrance for Sebastian?

52. Is it a strong, or a weak, point in that Olivia makes no comment when she learns that she has married an utter stranger? Are we to conclude that she was crazed by love, during the entire play?

53. How is Malvolio's plight recalled to Olivia?

54. What courtesy does Olivia extend to the Duke and Viola?

55. Whom did Sir Toby marry? Why?

56. Is it possible that Shakespeare invented the character of Malvolio as a warning to people not to take themselves so seriously? Granted this, what is sure to be the result?

57. Why is the Clown's song an appropriate ending to this play?

→ pouch w matches